D0098710

"There are a lot of elegant, sophisticated men in the world. And, God knows, there are plenty of talented musicians out there. You want handsome men? A dime a dozen. Surprisingly, there's also an abundance of courtly gentlemen walking among us. But if you want to read the autobiography of a courtly, handsome, urbane, gifted piano player, only one comes to mind and this is his story."

—**Alec Baldwin**, actor, filmmaker, and
New York Times bestselling author of *Nevertheless*

"It was a glorious wedding day in Waterford, Virginia. The prop jet carrying the orchestra could not land in the fog. Suddenly, on the hilltop, a miracle! The bandleader, Peter Duchin, flanked by his orchestra appeared in the mist like The Four Horsemen of the Apocalypse. They wore snappy tuxedos, their bowties loose like lariats. Duchin had his jacket slung over his shoulder on the crook of his finger, sprezzatura indeed.

Face the Music is a memoir by the maestro who accompanied Sinatra, played Capote's Black and White Ball, and entertained presidents. An outsider with a gift for inclusion, Duchin is equally at ease chatting with royalty or taking a meal in the hotel kitchen with the staff. Wherever he played, Duchin owned the joint. This is the story of how a stroke temporarily stopped the music, a broken heart led to a redeemed one, and the colorful characters who make his life a shimmering work of art also helped him heal. Written with the gifted Patricia Beard, this is a book for anyone who seeks strength, redemption, and wisdom. Candor and wit are the ebony and ivory of this splendid read. Duchin never gives up because there's always the next gig. Hallelujah!"

—**Adriana Trigiani**, *New York Times*
bestselling author of *The Shoemaker's Wife*

"There are so many reasons to admire Peter Duchin and his moving memoir. It's a victorious celebration of life filled with marquee names and stories, radioactive in their resonance. He knows how to live!"

—**Michael Feinstein**, singer, pianist, and founder of
The Great American Songbook Foundation

"Peter Duchin's eloquent meditation on his remarkable life hits all the right notes. A bewitching combination of wit and wisdom, heart and soul, and a story that touches and entertains, the book is captivating from start to finish. I didn't want it to end!"

—**Deborah Davis**, author of *Party of the Century: The Fabulous Story of Truman Capote and His Black and White Ball*

"In person, Peter Duchin lights up a room. His book is similarly luminous. Recounted with his signature charm, *Face the Music* thrums with humor, brio, and intelligence."

—**Peter Godwin**, author of *Mukiwa,* and
When a Crocodile Eats the Sun

"Inspiring and beautifully written. A journey through the highs and lows of a brilliant career, twice interrupted by life-threatening illnesses, which he overcame to return to the bandstand. What perils and triumphs! What a life!"

—**Philip K. Howard**, *New York Times* bestselling author
of *The Death of Common Sense*

FACE THE MUSIC

Also by Peter Duchin

Ghost of a Chance: A Memoir

A Musical Christmas with Peter Duchin

Good Morning, Heartache, A Philip Damon Mystery

Blue Moon, A Philip Damon Mystery

A MEMOIR

—

Face
the Music

PETER DUCHIN

with Patricia Beard

DOUBLEDAY
New York

All rights reserved. Published in the United States by Doubleday,
a division of Penguin Random House LLC, New York, and distributed
in Canada by Penguin Random House Canada Limited, Toronto.

www.doubleday.com

DOUBLEDAY and the portrayal of an anchor with a dolphin are
registered trademarks of Penguin Random House LLC.

Book design by Maria Carella
Jacket photograph © Ray Fisher / The LIFE Images
Collection/Getty Images
Jacket design by Michael J. Windsor

Library of Congress Cataloging-in-Publication Data
Names: Duchin, Peter, author. | Beard, Patricia, author.
Title: Face the music : a memoir / Peter Duchin, Patricia Beard.
Description: New York : Doubleday, 2021. | Includes bibliographical
references and index.
Identifiers: LCCN 2021014447 (print) | LCCN 2021014448 (ebook)
ISBN 9780385545877 (hardcover) | ISBN 9780385545884 (ebook)
Subjects: LCSH: Duchin, Peter. | Band directors—United
States—Biography.| Pianists—United States—Biography. |
LCGFT: Autobiographies.
Classification: LCC ML422.D8 A3 2021 (print) |
LCC ML422.D8 (ebook) | DDC 784.4—dc23
LC record available at https://lccn.loc.gov/2021014447
LC ebook record available at https://lccn.loc.gov/2021014448

MANUFACTURED IN THE UNITED STATES OF AMERICA

1 3 5 7 9 10 8 6 4 2
First Edition

For my wife, Virginia
&
My "barnacle," Adelle

Contents

CONTENTS

Introduction

FOR THE FIRST TIME since I had my stroke, I was going out beyond the physical therapy department at the hospital, and none of my clothes fit. My old khakis were huge. So was pretty much everything else in my closet. I had lost fifty-five pounds and shrunk from a size 44 to a 38.

It was the final day of an exhibition at the Frick Collection that I particularly wanted to see: two paintings on loan, a rare Rembrandt and *The Goldfinch* by Rembrandt's student Carel Fabritius. They would never be together again.

I was still using my walker, on the way to the relative independence of a cane, and a friend who worked at the museum understood that I couldn't safely navigate the crowd that would gather for a last look. She had arranged for my wife, Virginia, and me to visit before the doors opened to the public, and *I was going*. I threaded a silk necktie through the belt loops of the khakis, cinched it tightly to hold up my pants, tied it in a knot, and I was ready.

We entered through the basement and took the elevator up to the main floor. Except for a couple of guards and the woman who had organized our private view, we were on our own, in the presence of "old friends": I'd been visiting the Frick all my life.

The Goldfinch was the great surprise. The canvas measures only about 13" x 9," but even from across the room, the image of the bright-eyed bird chained to a perch has an arresting power. That painting was the engine of Donna Tartt's best-selling novel, and later the movie by the same name.

We made our way through the galleries, acquainting ourselves with works we hadn't spent time with before. Having the art more or less to ourselves was an extraordinary opportunity, and I thought of Henry Clay Frick, who lived in that house and often sat alone in those rooms after dinner to enjoy his collection.

When it was time to leave, we rode back to the basement and stepped out onto a ramp leading to the street. A line of people waiting for the museum to open stretched around the corner. I had gotten about halfway up the ramp when I felt the tie around my waist sliding loose, and my trousers heading south toward my knees. I warned Virginia, who was just behind me, "We've got a problem, darling," but before she could haul up my pants, the tie let go and I was standing there, shivering in my boxers. The folks in the line were treated to a spectacle that was flagrantly not a Rembrandt.

I looked at my audience, and called out as cheerfully as I could, "I doubt this is the show you came to see." We were all laughing, as Virginia dragged my pants up toward my waist, clutched them from behind, and we staggered off to hail a cab.

━━━

The stroke was my second close call. I was born with a life-threatening collapsed lung, and lived in an oxygen tent for my first year. All I can remember from that long-ago time is the soothing hum of the oxygen machine.

Seventy years later, in 2013, my lungs betrayed me again. I had had a bad case of pneumonia, but thought I'd recovered. Virginia and I went to the theater and out to dinner. I felt okay until, in a taxi on the way home, I had a crushing pain in my chest. This was *not* indigestion. The pain persisted, then increased. At two in the morning, Virginia took me to the emergency room at New York-Presbyterian/Weill Cornell Medical Center, a place I would come to know too well.

I was diagnosed with a clogged lung, and scheduled for "routine surgery"—as though invading the body with a scalpel and the rest of it could ever be "routine."

When I awakened from the anesthetic, I tried to move my arms. Nothing doing. To turn my head: nega-tive. Doctors and nurses hovered. I wanted to know what was wrong, but I couldn't speak. One of the doctors leaned over and told me that I had had a stroke and was being transferred to the intensive care unit. I had no idea what he was talking about.

Two months in the hospital; and I was finally released, and returned home. Virginia had set up a bed for my recovery in my office and library, which adjoined our bedroom through a bathroom, so she could hear me if I needed her. The room was crammed with books, and photographs of my mother, who died when I was six days old; and my father, Eddy Duchin, the celebrated bandleader, who became an instant star at the fabulous Central Park Casino in 1932. Dad died of leukemia at the age of forty-one. I became an orphan when I was twelve.

I like to imagine that if my father hadn't died so young, the Eddy Duchin Orchestra might have been playing at the Waldorf's Starlight Roof, just as I was starting my career as the bandleader and pianist at the St. Regis hotel's chic Maisonette.

Wherever I've lived, I've brought those photos with me. Lying in bed with little else to do, I decided to try to get to know my parents better, to see them as more than the family I didn't have.

I had unintentionally embarked on what would become a critical aspect of my recovery. Thinking deeply about my parents would lead me to reexamine old assumptions, and I began to consider the choices I'd made throughout my career as a bandleader, during an era when live music and dancing were a very big deal. I had a few surprises coming.

I ransacked boxes of memorabilia I'd stored and forgotten about: record albums, more photographs, private letters, newspaper and magazine clips. I even found a "once-upon-a-time" story written long after the event, describing my mother's great-aunt Tessie Oelrichs's 1904 White Ball in Newport, "the party of the season." In those days, bandleaders were almost never mentioned in the articles that enumerated every other detail of those Gilded

Age events, down to the quantity of the flowers, the exotic lands they came from, and the livery of the footmen.

A 1930 magazine featured a sixteen-page, fully illustrated article about the Central Park Casino, where New York's elite dined and danced to Dad's music. The story didn't mention that the enormously popular Mayor Jimmy Walker ran a mob-connected enterprise upstairs.

In the welter of papers, I came upon a 1946 telegram from my father, Jimmy Stewart, and Cary Grant, inviting people to an impromptu black-tie party at a nightclub-cum-gambling-joint on Sunset Strip. They billed it "the party of the century." The war was over, folks were ready to celebrate, and guests came from all over the country. At four in the morning, Hoagy Carmichael and Dad took turns at the piano, while Bing Crosby sang.

A lot of the stuff I'd saved related to the career I began in 1962, when I was twenty-six, leading my own band from the piano at the Maisonette. My father had been dead for over a decade, but plenty of people had listened to him on the radio, bought his records, or been lucky enough to dance to his music; and the 1956 tear-jerker film, *The Eddy Duchin Story,* kept his name alive. In no small part thanks to that recognition, I became part of the last era when bandleaders were considered celebrities.

By the time I started my post-stroke excavation, I'd played at thousands of events in forty-eight of the fifty states, Europe, Japan, South Africa, and the White House.

There was a lot to look at. And even more to think about. I've seen some of the damnedest things anyone could imagine.

Invitations to events featuring the Peter Duchin Orchestra were mixed in with others for private parties, engraved on heavy card stock. I discovered a 1974 Christmas catalog from Sakowitz, then Houston's most luxurious specialty store, offering "Gifts of Knowledge." Among them were "Piano Lessons from Peter Duchin (two lessons for $3,750)." In the photo, my younger son, Colin, who was around four years old, stands by the piano watching while I bend over the keyboard, looking serious, and hopefully worth the price. Evidently, someone thought I was: a woman in New York bought the lessons, and I went over to her apartment for the first one. When she opened the door, I saw that she was "dressed for company," in a rather sheer bathrobe. Not quite what I had expected, but I gave her the first lesson, but she skipped the second one. The others in the catalog were pretty interesting: there were two "Lessons on How to Fly a Spacecraft" from astronaut Walter Cunningham at $65,000; and "Lessons in Conversation with Truman Capote" ($3,000). Another discovery: in the intervening decades, my price went up—a lot. In 1999, the Dallas store Neiman Marcus, whose Christmas catalog was famous for *its* outrageously expensive gifts, offered an "Original Composition by Peter Duchin for $35,000." No sale.

I pulled out an old, buckled issue of *Town & Country,* with me on the cover. Another sheaf of clips "told all" (although definitely not *quite* all) about Truman Capote's Black and White Ball, for which Truman had asked me to play.

I had gotten used to being called a Society Bandleader, and described as "glamorous." I've never liked the tags, but that's how people thought about my father and me; and who they wanted us to be. I don't know how Dad felt, although, from his modest background as the son of Eastern European Jewish immigrants, I'd guess he was surprised, and I hope delighted, until he became so famous that the words lost their luster. It would take nearly half a century before the notion of "Society" would begin to transform and recede, and reports of deb parties, weddings, and charity balls fed fewer and fewer fantasies.

An enormously successful movie producer, rather modestly I thought, once told me he was in "the transportation business," taking people on thrilling rides from reality to dreams. Like him, although in a much lesser way, that's what I tried to do. My first night at the Maisonette, I began by playing "Make Someone Happy." I still often start a set with that tune, as we get the evening under way.

I've led my life on both sides of the bandstand. My mother was a famous debutante, and my father, of course, was a legendary musician. As Dad was on the road with his band, and then in the Navy during World War II, I rarely saw him until I was eight. I was brought up by Marie Harriman, my mother's dearly loved schoolmate; and her husband, Averell, diplomat, ambassador, advisor to presidents, and governor of New York. I went to Hotchkiss, one of the top New England prep schools, then to Yale. Musicians customarily approach the bandstand through the back door; I was just as likely to be having dinner with the guests before I took my place at the piano.

All this gave me a unique perspective on a distinctive time in the history of nightlife, music, and dancing.

I looked at the memorabilia I'd accumulated and asked myself what it added up to—not just my career, but the world I've been part of, and which is part of me.

I had plenty to think about, and plenty to write.

———

In 2020, with the stroke behind me, I was at the piano again, doing gigs with my band, managing to compensate for a left hand that hadn't fully recovered. We had been hired for a 100th birthday party in Memphis, scheduled for April 4. It would have been a great gig.

As we were making the final arrangements, we began to hear about a dangerous new virus that had started to spread. The party was canceled.

I couldn't have played anyway.

On March 22 I was in an ambulance, on the way back to the hospital with a serious case of Covid-19. I was intubated and sedated for forty-seven days. The odds I would make it were so slim, a rumor went around that I had died.

For the third time, my lungs threatened my survival.

And for the third time, I came out on the side of life.

———

STRICKEN

"Illness is the night-side of life, a more onerous citizenship. Everyone who is born holds dual citizenship, in the kingdom of the well and in the kingdom of the sick. Although we all prefer to use only the good passport, sooner or later each of us is obliged, at least for a spell, to identify ourselves as citizens of that other place."

—Susan Sontag, *Illness as Metaphor*

A portrait from the summer of 2018.
Photograph by Jonathan Morse

CHAPTER ONE

A Stroke
of Bad Luck

Afloat

I WAS HANGING ON to a railing to keep from falling over-board into the filthy Seine. I had somehow made it back to my beloved barge, after a wild mixture of jazz, pot, and booze, a night I vaguely remembered. The constant jolt of the barge bumping against the quay and the lap-ping of the waves nauseated me, and I was irritated by the raucous sound of the seagulls. I opened one eye and squinted against the sun blasting on my face, but the light came from a lesser sun, a large industrial lamp above my head. I was lying on a gurney in a bone-white room. My scream for help—the seagull sound—was silent. I could hear a conversation between a gray-haired man in a white coat with a stethoscope dangling on his chest, and several white-clad women, but I couldn't understand them. Fifty years had passed since the last time I was on that barge.

The Middle of the Night

MY WIFE, VIRGINIA, AND I had been returning from a play and dinner at Orso, the popular Italian restaurant in the Theater District. Orso stays open late, because Broad-way actors often come in for dinner, sometimes before they've even taken off their stage makeup. In the cab, I suddenly felt a sharp pain on my left side. I pressed on my chest to try to ease the pain, and lurched out onto the street in front of our apartment building. Upstairs, when I eased myself into bed, I felt as though a fist was clenching my lung. I tried to roll over, but I could hardly breathe.

I have atrial fibrillation, "AFib," for short, which causes an irregular heart rhythm. Virginia and I were both afraid I was having a heart attack, but neither of us mentioned the possibility. Maybe we were trying to avoid scaring each other.

"I'm calling the doctor," she said.

"Don't bother him. It's the middle of the night."

Men don't complain.

Virginia tapped our doctor's number into her iPhone. When she hung up, she said, "We're going to the emergency room *now*."

My wife is organized, keeps her cool, and always appears to be under control, even when everything seems uncontrollable. She's also tall and slim, with dark hair, fair skin, knockout legs, and impossibly elegant posture. The way she stands and looks at anyone trying to get in her way makes it clear that she isn't kidding. If Virginia wants something important, she usually makes it happen. What she wanted now was for me to get help.

As we rode downstairs, I was practically doubled over. The large night doorman looks formidable, but he's polite and friendly. I'm a baseball fan, and he usually updates me on the Yankees and Mets scores, but it was late November, the season was over, and we were on to football. He unlocked the heavy front door, and stepped into the street to look for a taxi.

Our building overlooks the East River. It's as far east

as you can go in Manhattan, and traffic is pretty sparse. At night, good luck.

A lone taxi with a lit topknot finally meandered along. The doorman waved it down, and we were on our way to what would turn out to be a very long trip.

The ER was predictably busy. I was subjected to the usual drill: wheelchair into a curtained cubicle; lie on a gurney; vital signs taken; doctor comes in; doctor leaves. Nurse says the doctor will come back soon. He doesn't.

I still hadn't received a diagnosis in the morning, but I was moved into a nice room with a sofa, a sitting area, and a wide window that overlooked the river. Flowing water has always appealed to me, as I love to fish. To avoid thinking about what might be covered by the ooze and concrete blocks on the bottom, I imagined a monstrously large striped bass swimming by.

The surgeon who arrived to talk to me looked very young. His hair was such a bright red that I wondered if he'd been teased at school. I was in pain, he said, because of a blockage in my right lung. I needed an operation to clear it out, but they couldn't operate until I stopped taking the blood thinner that controls the AFib. If my blood was too thin, I could bleed out on the table. After I was off the medication for a few days, I would begin to clot, and he could operate.

While I waited, orderlies wheeled me through the halls for tests. I saw an open door to a room where doctors and nurses were frantically performing CPR on a patient, taking turns to press forcefully on his chest. I've heard that to get the heartbeat right, it helps to push in time to the rhythm of the Bee Gees' 1977 song "Stayin' Alive."

Other members of the team pinched the patient's nose closed and breathed into his mouth to force oxygen into his lungs. I asked the orderly what was going on. "Gunshot," he said. On the way back, I asked him what had happened. "Died," he said.

VERDI'S *REQUIEM*

THE DOCTORS DECIDED MY blood consistency was in balance, and they were ready to go. I was lying on the operating table when a man wearing a mask and scrubs leaned his face close to mine, as though he were about to tell me a secret. He briefly described the way I would feel as I went under, and remarked, "You're a musician. Think of a great piece of music." I suggested that Verdi's *Requiem* might be appropriate. He smiled, and after a couple of bars, I slipped into oblivion.

THE SUDDEN DEATH OF BRAIN CELLS

I WAS STILL UNCONSCIOUS when Virginia came into the recovery room, and saw that something was very wrong: my face was out of kilter and my jaw drooped. She asked one of the nurses to get help immediately. Doctors crowded in, diagnosed a severe stroke, and rushed me to the intensive care unit. The sooner a stroke is identified and treated, the better chance a patient has of recovering, and I was already in the hospital.

When I first awakened, I didn't understand what had happened. All I knew was that I was caught in a nest of tubes and plastic bags, with wires attached to my fingers, my arms, my legs, and my chest. That should have made it clear that something very bad was going on, but the idea of a stroke didn't register. I wasn't tracking much, except for the sound of a machine that constantly emitted an intensely irritating beep-beep, just off A-flat.

A doctor whose face was a blur came over to my bed. In a matter-of-fact tone, he explained about the stroke, and told me it had damaged the right side of my brain, and the left was also affected. Whichever part of the brain is most severely "stricken," the opposite side takes the hit. That meant that my left side was out of commission, and might never recover.

A stroke causes the sudden death of brain cells, due to the lack of oxygen caused by a blockage of blood flow to the brain, or the rupture of an artery. When I could understand more, I learned that the right hemisphere of the brain is sensory and absorbs feelings. The left is used for organization, language, understanding, and process. The corpus callosum is located between the hemispheres and transfers information between the two sides. If one side isn't fully functioning, it limits what the brain can instruct the body to do. Among the symptoms are loss of speech, weakness, and paralysis of one side of the body. I would learn that I had them all.

I tried to ask the doctor how serious my condition was, and how likely I was to recover, but I could only make meaningless noises.

Much later, I would contact neuroanatomist Jill Bolte Taylor, who described her own stroke and recovery in her memoir, *My Stroke of Insight*. Dr. Taylor was kind enough to take time from writing her next book to email me an explanation of how the kind of brain damage I suffered can affect a musician:

> Music is a great example of how our two hemispheres complement each other in function. When we methodically and meticulously drill our scales over and over again, when we learn to read the language of staff notations . . . we are tapping primarily into the skills of our left brain. Our right brain kicks into high gear when we are doing things in the present moment, like performing, improvising or playing by ear. . . . Playing an instrument requires precise bilateral motor skills, so both hemispheres are creating refined movement.

"The performance of music is a whole-brained activity," she wrote, and only one side of my brain was working.

Dr. Taylor also believes in the plasticity of the brain, and its ability to repair and replace its neural circuitry. That was her experience; I hoped it would be mine.

Yet for months—for years—as I recovered, one function eluded me. I couldn't ignite the part of the brain that sends messages to my left hand. Without two functioning hands, I would be deprived of my greatest pleasure; and my long career as a pianist and bandleader would be over.

With more than fifty years in the profession, I have a bursting "file cabinet" of music in my head, and I searched for a piece written solely for the right hand. The great pianist Leon Fleischer had a neurological condition, lost the use of his right hand for a time, and played concerti written for the left. Paul Wittgenstein, the older brother of the philosopher Ludwig Wittgenstein, had his right arm amputated after he was shot in the elbow during World War I. He commissioned some of the best composers of the era to write music he could perform. The most famous is Ravel's Concerto for the Left Hand.

For the right hand alone: nothing.

I was only conscious on and off, and sometimes I hallucinated.
The fantasy I liked best was that I was back in Paris on my
Yale junior year abroad, living on a barge on the Seine, and playing
on a junk shop piano.

CHAPTER TWO

Fugues, Dreams, and Hallucinations

The Lady in Black

IN THE EARLY DAYS after my stroke, I often couldn't tell the difference between reality—whatever that was— and dreams. After a week in the ICU, I was moved into a double room. As I was rolled in, I saw an old lady wearing a shapeless black dress. She was sitting in a chair on the side of the curtain that separated the patients, fingering a rosary, humming, or maybe praying in a language I couldn't identify. The man in the bed was coughing, with a horrible thick sound. I heard him again and again during the next days.

I never saw the lady in black again. Maybe I had been hallucinating. Was she a priestess, who could predict whether I would live or die?

I was wheeled past the woman who may or may not have been there. Nurses and orderlies heaved me onto the bed and placed a rolling machine under my feet to keep the circulation in my legs going. I could see the sheets moving and had a flash of the motels where I sometimes stayed when my band was on the road, places where you put a coin in a slot and the bed shakes and jiggles to give you a massage, or whatever.

A television was mounted high on the wall. To my relief, it wasn't turned on, but the screen saver showed a field of poppies. The image reminded me of the second act of the Metropolitan Opera's production of Wagner's *Parsifal,* the story of the search for the Holy Grail. I thought fondly of the great diva Jessye Norman, who stood an imposing 6'1." She was hardly a sylph, but she brilliantly gave the impression of tiptoeing through the poppies. In my mind I could hear the extraordinary music from that scene.

NUNS IN WHITE

NURSES BUSTLED AROUND, and after one of my many naps they seemed to briefly transform into nuns, like the ones I encountered in France when I was in college, bicycling through Europe with friends. We had found a pleasant stretch of grass to make camp for the night, unpacked our sleeping bags, and exhausted, we slept. At daylight, we were awakened by a cluster of white-clad nuns, standing over us and tittering: we had settled on the lawn of their convent. They took us up the hill to the chapter house, invited us in, and fed us breakfast. Unfortunately, they neglected to offer us much needed baths.

PARIS, 1956–57

SOMETIMES WHEN I WOKE up, I had to remind myself where I was. Maybe I was dying, and my life was flashing by. I wanted to slow down the reel and relive my time in France.

I was on my Yale junior year abroad, living on a barge

while I studied musicology in a private class, French at the Sorbonne, and political philosophy at Sciences Po, the famous Paris Institute of Political Sciences.

My music instructor was Andrée Vaurabourg, who had often played piano duets with her late husband, the pianist and composer Arthur Honegger. The Vaurabourg-Honeggers had an unusual arrangement: he insisted he would only marry her if they lived in separate apartments. He said he needed complete solitude when he was composing. That's one reason I'm not a composer: it's a lonely life, and I like to be with people.

Mme Vaurabourg was probably about sixty, and her fame had been well earned: Pierre Boulez, the composer and international conductor, was one of her students. She was selective, her classes were small, and her students were expected to annotate the score as she played a piece of music. I began to understand the great French composer, conductor, and teacher Nadia Boulanger's dictum: "A great work of art is made out of a combination of obedience and liberty."

I had bought the barge I was living on at a terrific bargain. I found it after my godmother, Ginny Chambers, who lived in the wonderful house she and her husband, Brose, had bought from Cole Porter, decided that I wasn't going to be their houseguest for the duration, and I needed someplace else to live. (Ginny did tell me that I could bring over my laundry, which I tried to do around lunchtime, in the hope that I'd be invited to join the guests, and I often was.) I was settled on the barge when my great friend George Plimpton suggested that I take a roommate. George was an American patrician with an East Coast drawl and an unparalleled sense of humor and adventure. He and some friends had founded what was then the fledgling literary magazine *The Paris Review*. George, who was planning to return to New York—eventually—hired Robert Silvers to replace him. Bob didn't have a place to live and George decided that my barge was the solution, and it was a fine one. Both of them would be ushers at my first wedding.

The Paris Review was Bob's entire focus: he didn't drink, ate moderately, and somehow managed to ignore the din of our nightly parties and jam sessions. I can still see him with his wonderfully infectious smile, gesturing with his hands, as he interviewed such literary luminaries as James Baldwin and Thornton Wilder over the noise of our music and laughter. The barge proved a suitable atmosphere for the burgeoning magazine.

We didn't have electricity or a phone, and people just dropped by. They walked over the gangplank from the quay, and night after night, friends, and friends of friends, turned up. We used Coleman lanterns and candles for light, while I played jazz on a dilapidated upright piano. Experienced musicians came to the barge for jam sessions, and I learned a lot from them. The Crazy Horse Saloon was nearby; I dated one of the dancers who worked there, and invited them to take their breaks with us. They were beautiful, seemingly often half-naked, and sexy.

GEORGE

PLIMPTON OFTEN SPENT A night or two with us, sleeping on an Army cot we found in the street. He was so tall his feet stretched over the end of the cot, but he was very interested in the Crazy Horse girls, which inspired him to camp with us. From time to time, he walked up the street to the Plaza Athénée, strolled into a sitting room, and used the hotel stationery to write his father: "Please send more money. It's very expensive here." Sometimes it worked.

George was a wonderful writer and a superb editor, but his unique quality was his ability to persuade people to let him try the apparently impossible, and then write about the experience. What he called "participatory journalism" would make him famous: pitching against professional baseball players at Yankee Stadium, and sparring three rounds with boxing greats Archie Moore and Sugar Ray Robinson on assignment for *Sports Illustrated*.

He also played with the New York Philharmonic orchestra. Leonard Bernstein, the conductor of the Philharmonic, was one of George's many friends, and he had asked Lenny if he would let him play the triangle on the orchestra's upcoming Canadian tour.

Lenny agreed that he could sit with the percussion section, in what was known as "the shady corner" at the back of the orchestra. His first go was in Winnipeg, where he struck the triangle with little effect. The next time, he tried sleigh bells, but chimed in too soon. That was enough. Lenny told George he'd had his last chance, but the other members of the percussion section had grown fond of him, and made the case that he should have one last try. His instrument was the gong, which came in near the end of the third movement of Tchaikovsky's joyful *Symphony No. 2 in C minor*. George was so determined to get it right that he hit the gong with stunning power. When a musician plays particularly well, the other members of the orchestra often shuffle their feet very quietly. George got a full shuffle. Later, he told me gleefully that when the concert was over Lenny came up to him and said, "No one has ever hit a gong quite that hard." After that, when Lenny wanted more impact from his musicians, he would say "Give me the Winnipeg sound."

The Philharmonic was not George's only musical adventure. One day, to my horror, he called to tell me he was planning to play the piano on Amateur Night at the Apollo Theater in Harlem and asked if I could teach him a couple of simple tunes. The theater had been the launching pad for some of the greatest musical stars, among them Sarah Vaughan, James Brown, Pearl Bailey, Buddy Holly and the Crickets, Stevie Wonder, Ella Fitzgerald, Charlie Barnett, Dionne Warwick, and Michael Jackson with the Jackson Five. Now George was going to appear on the same stage.

I went over to his apartment and showed him a few chords, which led to another, and then another, and another. The night of the performance, Bob Silvers and I waited anxiously in the first mezzanine. George walked onto the stage wearing his blue blazer and a striped tie. Looking confident, he settled on the piano stool, placed his hands in what he evidently thought was a professional position, and began playing the endless series of chords. I knew he'd be all right when I heard an older couple sitting behind us saying, "Far out!"

Many years later, George wrote modestly about his exploits, "I suppose in a mild way there is a lesson to be learned for the young, or the young at heart—the gumption to get out and try one's wings."

George died in 2003, ten years before I had my stroke. In the hospital and after, I wished for nothing more than for him to stop by, settle his lanky frame on a chair, with his legs stretched out and crossed at the ankle, and tell me another story.

ALL THAT JAZZ

THE FRENCH LOVED JAZZ, and when I lived there during my glorious junior year abroad, some of the top French and American jazz musicians were playing all over town. They were often more appreciated in Paris than in New York, and the Black musicians didn't have to face the same bigotry that limited their ability to go on tour in the U.S.

Bebop, a subgenre of jazz that incorporates influences from rhythm and blues, gospel music, and Dixieland, was in fashion. The music was hot and bold, musicians deconstructing and improvising, often on well-known melodies. The saxophonist Gary Giddins described the way they played as "the ultimate in rugged individualism. It's going out there on that stage and saying: It doesn't matter how anybody else did it. This is the way I'm going to do it."

In Paris, I could go to different clubs and hear good musicians every night, experimenting and playing the music the way they felt it. One night a few jazz musicians stopped by the barge with Allen Eager, the great jazz tenor and alto saxophonist. He was one of the early White musicians to play in Black bands; at that time, Black and White musicians didn't work together professionally. Allen and I became good friends, and often played together. He suggested rhythms and harmonies I had never thought about, but which eventually became second nature to me. Sometimes, we'd go to a club together; he'd introduce me to the other musicians and they'd let me sit in. I was intoxicated.

Allen's drug addiction shut down his career for a while, and he turned to serious auto racing—his mother had taught him to drive when he was nine, after she caught him driving a garbage truck at the Catskill resort his parents owned. He was back at music in the 1980s, touring with Charles Mingus and Chet Baker, but by then we'd lost touch.

Of course, I was also obligated to keep up with my studies to get credit for my junior year at Yale, but Paris, jazz, and the world of the barge were irresistible distractions.

Much later, Wynton Marsalis, the trumpet player, composer, and creative director of Jazz at Lincoln Center, described what I felt then, and still do. "Jazz music celebrates life—human life," he said. "The range of it. The absurdity of it. The ignorance of it. The greatness of it. The intelligence of it. The sexuality of it. The profundity of it. And it deals with all of it. It deals with it."

The great pianist Jelly Roll Morton, the first to write down jazz music and make it available beyond its birthplace in New Orleans, explained, jazz is "a *style,* not compositions. Any kind of music may be played in jazz."

Many jazz musicians believe, as Duke Ellington did, that "the United States of America spawned certain ideals of freedom and independence through which, eventually

jazz was evolved, and the music is so free that many people say it is the only unhampered, unhindered expression
of complete freedom yet produced in this country."

Until I lived in Paris, I had done what was expected
of me in a narrow, if privileged world. With jazz, I found
a freedom I had never known.

My father had never been attracted to jazz, which had
appealed to me from an early age. Dad knew how I felt
and once, as a joke, he autographed a piece of paper "To
Peter, from Fats Waller." It took me a while to realize that
I could play the same kind of music as my father did, with
a jazzy feeling and create my own style.

I lived with Marie and Averell Harriman until I was nine years
old, while my father was on the road with the Eddy Duchin Band,
and then in the Navy. Dad came to see me one summer day,
and Marie, Dad, and I got together in the Harrimans'
garden for a photograph.

CHAPTER THREE

Alone

A Soppy Mess

THE DAY I WAS moved into a private room on the sixteenth floor of the hospital, I'm almost sure I heard one of
the smiling nurses say, "Welcome home, Mr. D.," before
they cleared out.

I wondered how many people had lain in the same
bed, and if they had recovered, or died right there. That
was pretty damn depressing. Being alone was not what I
needed.

December was approaching, darkness fell early, snow
obscured the view from my window, and I felt closed off
from a world that was carrying on without me. To my surprise, I started to sob. Even when I was very young, I kept
my feelings to myself. Without the unconditional love of
parents, I always felt that I needed to please, to be liked. I
figured that no one cares for a kid who cries when he falls
down and scrapes his knees, or if his feelings are hurt.
Like a swimmer who encounters an unexpected undertow,
I always fought my way back to shore, dried myself off,
and moved on. This was different.

Soon I was a soppy mess. My face was wet, my nose
was dripping, and the top of my hospital gown and sheets
were damp. A tissue box was on a tray table on the left
side of the bed, but I couldn't use that hand to reach it.

I had cried that way when I heard that Bobby Kennedy was killed. I'd seen him only a couple of days earlier, when I was campaigning for him in California.

I cried when Marie Harriman died. She was as close to a mother as I had had, and a link to my real mother. Harry and Nancy Whitney, the children from her prior marriage, confided that she was more maternal with me than with them.

Another devastating loss was when my black Lab, Malcolm, developed cancer and had to be put down. I've had a lot of dogs and loved them all, but I loved Malcolm the most. That day, I walked into the woods near our house, sobbed for hours, and only returned at dusk. Malcolm was a member of the family I had always wanted, and that I'd finally found with my first wife, Cheray, and our children.

For a long time, Cheray and I were a great team. From the night of our wedding reception, when my band alternated with Count Basie's, we had a terrific time. I trusted her opinions and instincts about people and jobs, and before our first child, Jason, was born, she often traveled with me. We knew people all over; we were often invited to stay with them, and it was fun to mix visits with work.

After Jason, came our daughter, Courtnay, and we decided to move to the country about an hour from New York. We were building a tall, light-filled house, and one day Jackie and Ari Onassis drove out to see how we were coming along. To our astonishment, Ari asked the contractor for a ladder, climbed up, sat on a beam and gazed out to admire the view.

We had become friends with Jackie, whose mother had been a classmate of my mother's; and of course, I had worked for Bobby Kennedy and knew Bobby and Ethel well. When Jackie moved to New York, Cheray and I spent a lot of time with her. She was always pestered by paparazzi, and when I could, I stood in front of her, blocked their view, and tried to look threatening. It didn't always work, but it helped.

Jackie once made a remark to me, which I've puzzled over: "You and I will always be outsiders," she said, but she didn't elaborate. Over the years I've had various theories about what she meant. Certainly, one was that even though her stepfather, Hugh Auchincloss, was a member of a distinguished old family, his name and legacy were not hers. And I certainly was not a Harriman.

Fame also ensures that one will be treated differently—turned into another kind of outsider. Perhaps that's what she was thinking about.

Once our house was finished and we moved in, we had our third child, Colin, and I thought we were happy. In a summer photograph from that time, Cheray and I are sitting on chaises near our pool. Cheray's little Norwich terrier, Nutkin, is trying to lick her face, and she's turning away and laughing, with her blond hair sweeping down the side of the chaise. I'm stretched out, with Malcom lying near me, looking and feeling as contented and happy as I've ever been. It is still heartbreaking to look at that picture.

If I had been wiser, I would have realized that despite days like those, I was away too much, and our team was fraying. Cheray understood that I was traveling to do my job and support our family, but she was lonely. We'd been married for eighteen years when she decided she'd had enough. I was devastated when she left, but I eventually moved on. We're still such good friends that, forty years later, we talk to each other every couple of days.

Painting My Room with Music

MY SOLACE IS PLAYING or listening to music. At times, I can "paint" a space with sound. I see colors when I hear music: loud and agitated passages are often red; soft and moody are blue. Duke Ellington also saw music and colors together, a syndrome that's known as sound-to-color synesthesia. That night in my single room, the music was silent, and the colors had faded to dark.

Two People I Hardly Knew
and a Dog

IN THE HOSPITAL, I listened to music of all sorts. I wish that had been true when I was nine years old. Instead of music, I had a dog. Everything considered, he was a pretty good consolation for a very confused kid.

Dad had been honorably discharged from the Navy at the end of the war. Like many others who fought in the Pacific, he stopped in Hawaii on the way home. When he was there earlier, he met Chiquita Winn, a tall, attractive (and married) woman. By the time he returned to Hawaii, she was a widow, and of course, he was a widower. He courted her, brought her back to New York, and they were married at Averell and Marie's townhouse.

Chiquita was half-Spanish and half-English, the daughter of a prominent British diplomat. Maybe because she had grown up in a formal international world, she tended to maintain a polite distance. Even when I was an adult and we became friends, I never quite achieved real intimacy with her. She always seemed rather remote, which wasn't great, because my new home would be with her and Dad.

Dad and Chiquita had barely settled into their house on Long Island when all of our lives entered a phase for which none of us was prepared. My father and the Harrimans assumed that once Dad was settled, I would live with him. My suitcases were packed, and I was abruptly moved from my cozy room at Arden, the Harrimans' estate fifty miles north of Manhattan, to Manhasset, Long Island. I don't think anyone told me I was leaving for good until the Harrimans' driver brought me to a place I'd never seen, to live with two people I barely knew. I've tried again and again, but I can't remember leaving Arden, a word that still sounds like Eden. I can't even bring up an image of arriving at my father's house.

Chiq had never had children, and I'm sure she didn't know what to expect when she became the stepmother of an angry eight-year-old who wanted to have his father to himself. She and Dad tried to connect with me, but it took a while. The ice-breaker was a taffy-colored cocker spaniel puppy named Gyp, short for gypsy; I think the name came from a book I'd read. Gyp slept on my bed, and I started to feel more comfortable, and comforted.

Thinking about Gyp from the hospital, I longed for my current dog, Harper. She's small, short-legged, and yellowish, half-Pomeranian and half something else. Like my other dogs, she sleeps with me, scrunches around to make herself snug, sighs, snores, and we doze off together. One reason I felt so sad and alone was that I missed my dog.

Harper isn't the only pet that liked to burrow into my bed. Several years ago, I had two parrots: a small, stocky caique named Igor; and Sahib, an Alexandrine Ringneck. They would push the covers back, settle under the bedding, and make a kind of nest. One of my kids said, "What are you going to get next? A falcon?"

"Why not?" I said.

"Someone to Watch Over Me"

THE WOMAN WHO WOULD become my consolation, caretaker, and friend arrived shortly after I had been moved to a private room. Virginia had to go back to work, and she set out to find "someone to watch over me," a phrase I've always liked, from the tune Ira and George Gershwin wrote in 1926.

The challenge was to find a competent, pleasant, and experienced advocate. I didn't need a trained nurse, but I did need someone who knew what she was doing, who wouldn't take any crap from me, act as my advocate, track how I was coming along, and keep me company. Virginia wasn't going to settle for a person who spent her days talking on her cell phone and chewing gum. The plan was for me to recover, not to be driven crazy.

Adelle Dyett made the cut and showed up in the doorway of my room two weeks after I had my stroke, just in time for Thanksgiving.

A tall, striking woman from Trinidad in her early

forties, Adelle is smart, professional, has a great sense of humor and a careful eye. She had taken care of children and elderly patients, and been around enough seriously ill people to recognize when things looked bad. She later confessed that when she first saw me, "I thought for sure you were a goner," but she was determined that I wouldn't be "going" if she could help it. She arrived at the hospital every morning, and left at the end of the day; wheeled me around and wheedled me to get my act together when I didn't like the food, the physical therapy, the hospital schedule, and most of all what seemed to be my nearly unconquerable limitations.

Once we got to know each other, we started to tease each other. I'd tell her I'd buy her a one-way ticket back to Trinidad, and she would accept. She says she's still waiting. Eight years later, Adelle has become my personal assistant, health advocate, and pal: if I don't feel or look right, she's on the case—but first, we had to get to know each other. That had a few roadblocks, one being that I still couldn't talk well enough to make myself understood.

THE SNOW GLOBE

I WAS FACING A cheerless Christmas when one of my friends stopped by the hospital for a short visit, which was about as much as I could take at that point. As she left, she handed me a package and skipped out the door. Inside the wrapping was a snow globe, which, oddly, looked as bleak as I felt. A pile of snow was huddled at the bottom of the glass, but that seemed to be all. No faux Austrian village, no Santa, no Three Kings or shepherds with their lambs. I shook the dome, the snow whirled, and the word FUCK! appeared in large red capital letters. If I could have moved, I would have fallen out of bed laughing.

Adelle is deeply religious, goes to church every Sunday and sings in the choir. She would not have been amused, at least not then. She eventually got accustomed to my salty expressions, but she still keeps her language clean. No one is going to wash out Adelle Dyett's mouth with soap, not ever.

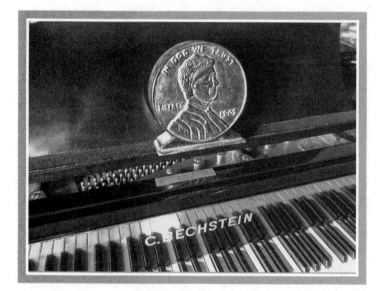

If I ever wanted to play the precious Bechstein that had belonged
to my father again, I would have to rehabilitate my left hand.
My first exercise was to pick up a penny and drop it into the
slot in this penny bank. It sounded simple. It wasn't.

▬

CHAPTER FOUR

Zero
Out of Ten

▬

"You'd Better Talk
to the Devil Yourself"

THE LONG HOSPITAL DAYS didn't feel as empty after a friend downloaded selections from his extraordinary library of music on an iPhone. With very few distractions, except when a nurse came in to take my vital signs, I had the luxury of time, and chose several works, listened carefully and repeatedly, got to know them well, and analyzed them.

It's fortunate that I'm a musician, because, as the science writer and author Kayt Sukel writes, "Music is known to extensively activate the human brain to recover by helping to restore the blood vessels and synaptic connections damaged by stroke. . . . Music listening induces activation in the pleasure and reward systems in the brain . . . [and enhances] cognitive, emotional and neural recovery."

As I wrote in my first memoir, *Ghost of a Chance,* "Listening to Bach, I felt a great ordering of things. Everything I had been straining to understand about music suddenly fit together. The harmonies, the bass lines, the rhythms—all confusions were resolved." That is still true.

While I analyzed Beethoven's late string quartets and the Prokofiev piano sonatas, wishing I could play them, I thought about how different musicians and conductors interpret the same works. In Salzburg, I heard Herbert von Karajan conducting Richard Strauss's *Der Rosenkavalier*. Two nights later, I was at the opera in Vienna when Carlos Kleiber conducted the same opera. One version was forty-five minutes longer than the other.

A very cool nurse, part of the cadre I had begun to call "the militia," sometimes came in when I was listening to a passage I didn't want to miss. I was in the midst of Berlioz's *The Damnation of Faust* when she turned up. The opera had reached the critical moment when Mephistopheles is tempting Faust. I asked her to leave me alone, because "The Devil is bargaining with a deeply troubled man." Her response: "Well then, you'd better talk to the Devil yourself."

Doctors stopped by each day, usually with a flock of residents in their wake. They removed the top of my pajamas, listened to my heartbeat and lungs, took my blood pressure, and described what I had, and what they had observed. They treated me kindly, as though I was their only patient, showing the residents a comforting bedside manner. Meanwhile, I showed them what a bored patient was like.

After one of those visits, I had put in my earbuds and was paying rapt attention to a Mozart piano sonata when a young resident came back. "I hear you're a musician," he said. "What were you listening to?" I told him, and he said, rather superciliously, "I bet you've never heard of Led Zeppelin." I remarked that, curiously enough, I dig Led Zeppelin, often play "Stairway to Heaven," and suggested that he might consider trying Mozart.

SCRAMBLED EGGS

MY APPETITE BEGAN TO return, but I wasn't allowed to eat solid food until the swallowing reflex in my esophagus began to work again; if it wasn't functioning, the food would go into my lungs. My meals mostly consisted of Ensure, Jell-O, applesauce, and an unidentifiable mush. The large Haitian nurse who usually brought my food would appear in the doorway and announce "Here I am!" She would set the tray on the table that swiveled over the bed, open the lid over the plate, look at the contents and ask wickedly, "Are you actually gonna eat this stuff?"

"I'm not really hungry," I'd say. "Why don't you eat it instead?" She'd make an exaggerated face, and retort, "Are you kidding?" Despite the menu, I was always glad to see her. If she had time, she'd stay for a bit to chat. Being on her feet all day must have been tiring, and sometimes she settled into a chair for a little while. I once asked her if she knew how to do voodoo. She said she didn't, but her brother did. I was tempted to suggest that he come by for a professional visit.

I was regularly tested to gauge how my swallowing was coming along. When the doctors finally decided I was ready to try something modestly more solid, another nurse appeared with a plate of scrambled eggs. I had stored away a bottle of Tabasco sauce for just that moment, and doused the eggs before the nurse spooned them into my mouth. Some dribbled out the left side, where I didn't have any feeling. At least the stroke hadn't affected my taste buds, and I thought longingly about the smoked salmon and other delicacies that well-meaning pals had sent (and often enjoyed when they visited me, while I looked on with envy).

Some of the friends who came by didn't know what to say to me when they saw my condition. My words were barely intelligible; and if I started a sentence, I often couldn't remember where I was headed. Friends who realized I couldn't speak clearly and weren't sure if I understood them often looked away and talked to each other. Other pals treated me as though nothing had changed. That was strange, too.

I began speech therapy, blowing out my cheeks, sticking out my tongue, and making faces. I suggested to the therapist that a great exercise would be trying to suck in spaghetti, but that wasn't part of the program. My older son, Jason, a teacher who started his own school in the Bronx, showed me a fabulous app that included everything Shakespeare wrote, and suggested that I read the plays out loud. I downloaded it on my iPad, and started with *King Lear,* which seemed quite appropriate. Jason kept me company, sitting in one of the hospital chairs that seem designed to discourage visitors from staying too long. If I stumbled over words and forgot what some of them meant, we laughed, and I kept trying. Reading to myself was a trial as well. Virginia brought me newspapers and magazines every day, and I tried to read them. I understood the sentences, but by the time I turned a page, the meaning had fled.

Sometimes I felt chilly, and my younger son, Colin, who looks a lot the way I did when I was younger, brought me a plaid camp blanket and a wool cape. One day, he turned up with an electric razor to shave off the makings of my nascent beard. Although I thought it made me look rather up-to-date, when I could move around and could shave myself for the first time, with Colin's help, I was exhilarated. Even the smallest step toward recovery meant more than I could have imagined.

My daughter, Courtnay, a psychologist who lives in Bozeman, Montana, came to New York when I had my stroke, and stayed as long as she could. After she returned to her family and her practice, she called every day, asked what I was thinking about, and offered useful advice about how to cope with the depression that often accompanies a stroke. She reminded me that I had always been optimistic. She was right on that count, but I was very frustrated.

"We'll Darn Well Do It"

I'D BEEN LYING IN bed like a lump, and I was desperate to get moving, but I wasn't sure how much progress I could make. My score on the test that measured the muscles in my left arm from my shoulder to my fingertips was zero, and I ranked below the normal cutoff for my age in cognitive ability. The task of getting me back into some sort of shape—whatever that would mean—fell to Dan Trufaro, a wiry young man with spiky dark hair and a friendly expression. He didn't look like a weightlifter, and I couldn't even hoist myself into a sitting position on my own, but Dan was an athlete. He had tried out for a big-league baseball team, didn't get the nod, and instead trained as a physical therapist. He would be able to cart me around with ease.

I told him that my most important objective was to

achieve enough mobility in my left arm and shoulder to play the piano with both hands. "Very ambitious," he said, "but we'll darn well do it." He hauled me more or less upright against the pillows, and within a couple of days he could carry me to a chair, then help me into a wheelchair, and Adelle could wheel me up to the therapy gym. I had been confined to my room for so long that even being in the hall felt good.

A sign inside the gym read "What Is Your Goal Today?" I had plenty of goals. The idea of choosing only one at a time was a relief.

PICKING UP PENNIES

MY FIRST TASK IN rehab was to pick up pennies and put them in the slot in a large bronze penny-shaped piggy bank. I tried to slide them or flick them, and I was tempted to use my right hand and get it over with, but I slowly improved.

Another frustrating fine motor exercise involved snapping clothespins onto a wire. The pins were different colors, indicating which required the most strength and coordination. I hope I never have to use a clothespin again.

I wonder who thought up this one: to improve my balance, a therapist named Rebecca, who had been a serious gymnast, attached me to a harness to keep me upright, and guided me into a three-sided cardboard "room." The floor moved up and down and sideways, and the walls moved in and out. It's lucky I don't get seasick.

The great mystery was a mirror in a small box with an opening for my left hand and a divider that prevented me from seeing the mirror on the outside. I tapped out a simple tune on a table with my right hand, and using some kind of muscle memory, the left, which was in the box, started to mimic the right. It appeared that part of my brain and my left hand were connecting, but when the exercise was over, the hand was flat and floppy again.

At the Starting Gate

THE OTHERS IN THE gym were strangers, but not for long. Before we began our workouts, the therapists lined up our wheelchairs in a row, like horses at the starting gate. Some of us got to know each other, and after a while a few patients began to confide in me. They talked about their fears and told me about themselves. I understood how they felt: I was learning what it was like to be deprived of a major part of a life.

Patients who had seen *The Eddy Duchin Story,* which came out in 1956 when I was still at Yale, joked about my "Mom," played by Kim Novak at the height of her career. There were many inaccuracies in the movie, but overall, watching it was both moving and weird.

It made sense that Tyrone Power was chosen to play Dad; they were friends and looked more or less alike; and the beautiful Kim Novak did a surprisingly good job playing my mother, whom she had never met.

Yet, I left the movie theater feeling confused, sad, angry, and exploited. Toots Shor, Dad's great buddy, and one of my surrogate fathers, had come along to keep me company. Toots, who owned the restaurant by the same name, had the height and heft of the bouncer he'd once been, the sense of humor of a good stand-up comic, and the loyalty that attracted the athletes and movie stars who considered his unpretentious restaurant their personal hangout. Dad had offered to back him, and gave him a blank check to fill in when he needed it. Toots never cashed the check; he framed it instead. His friendships were wide and sometimes surprising. In 1959, when he opened in a new location, his close friend then–Chief Justice Earl Warren was photographed holding a shovel of dirt.

As we left the dark theater and walked out into the sunlight, Toots knew I was upset. Anyone in my position would have been. Toots asked me:

"When were you born?"

"July."

"When was the boy in the film born?"

"New Year's Eve."

"Yeah," he said. "If they had to make *that* up, how much else do you think was true?"

One of the guys in rehab who had seen the film said he wouldn't blame me if I had an Oedipus complex. I wasn't thinking about Greek tragedies when I got to know Kim. I was in college when I heard the movie was shooting in Central Park, and I turned up to surprise my on-screen mother. We went out to dinner that night with a couple of my friends, who had come along to meet the star. After that, Kim and I continued to see each other. She was only four years older than I was, but sometimes I teased her and called her "mother." Our friendship lasted long enough that it made it into the gossip columns. I've often been asked the obvious question, but I've avoided answering. I don't usually mention Ava Gardner, either.

OTHER "GUESTS"

YOU NEVER KNOW WHOM you'll run into in the hospital. "Run" was hardly the right word in my case, but three people I knew were also in therapy: the eternally beautiful Deeda Blair, a philanthropist with a special interest in medicine, had been hit by a car and eventually recovered. The late Buck Henry, cowriter of *The Graduate,* codirector of *Heaven Can Wait,* and the smart, funny host of *Saturday Night Live* during its first five seasons, had also had a stroke. His humor was notably damped down, and would never fully return. And there was my college friend Peter Beard, the brilliant photographer, artist, writer, intrepid African adventurer, whose fame was enhanced by the gorgeous women he dated and married. Peter had also had a pretty severe stroke.

In the most famous picture of Peter, he has squirmed into the body of a crocodile he had just shot. His head and arms are outside the croc's jaws, and he's writing in his diary. The picture doesn't show that the croc's body continued to contract, even after death. It squeezed so hard that it broke a couple of Peter's ribs.

Peter was indomitably independent and liked to do things his own way. After his stroke, although he was so confused that he had to ask a niece to remind him how to use his camera, he checked himself out of the hospital. He said he didn't like the medications the doctors were giving him. He preferred his own, which the doctors didn't prescribe.

MY LEFT HAND

MANY WEEKS INTO PHYSICAL therapy, Dan asked if I wanted to try to play the upright piano in the visitors' waiting room. He warned me that someone had donated it about ten years earlier, and it probably hadn't been tuned since.

I usually play a baby grand, but I don't always get to choose the piano, or its condition. One client who was giving a dance in a barn hadn't used the instrument for a while, and when I opened the lid, a mouse scurried off. Another time, I sat down at an old upright at a house in Florida and a toad hopped out.

Now I was in a dingy room with an instrument that probably wouldn't sound great, but I didn't care. I sat on the stool, placed my hands on the keys, and nervously began. My right hand was fine, and the left automatically dropped into the correct position, but it barely moved, and it couldn't follow a tune I had played a hundred times. After the mirror box exercise, I had been irrationally hopeful, and I was bitterly disappointed. I had to remind myself that I *had had a stroke*. Of course, I was still struggling.

Dan agreed that when I left the hospital, he would come to the apartment to continue my therapy as an outpatient, and bring new tasks for me to perform. I had a flash of empathy with my dog Harper: I repeatedly ask her to give me her paw—which she won't. Nor does she sit when I ask her to.

Members of the band came to visit me and reminded me of the
way it feels to launch into the lively and sometimes rather unusual
evenings like those we've shared over the decades.

Photograph by Jonathan Morse

CHAPTER FIVE

The Happy
Chemical

"You Want Us to Play Something for You, Boss?"

MEMBERS OF THE BAND occasionally came to visit, and asked, "You want us to play something for you, boss?" That would have been great, but it would have shaken the hell out of the rest of the floor. Instead, I told them that maybe when I recovered, we could come back dressed in scrubs and give an afternoon concert for the nurses. It was an amusing idea, but it never happened.

I've heard that laughter releases serotonin, sometimes called "the happy chemical" because it contributes to feelings of well-being and cheer. The band provided plenty of that on their visits, reminding me of amusing or bizarre incidents we'd experienced together. They kidded me about women who were looking for an intimate chat, and came over while I was playing, sat down next to me on the bench and made an extravagant gesture, sometimes spilling a drink into the piano. Those close encounters are one reason I prefer to sit on a chair or a stool when I play. I've even had folks lean over and inadvertently snap the piano cover closed, threatening to crush my fingers.

My vocalist, guitarist, and sidekick, Roberta Fabiano, draws cartoons about some of our gigs, focusing on the unexpected and often hilarious moments she has observed during the forty years we've been working together, and she brought along a spiral notebook with a collection for me to look at. One image shows a newspaper ad for the Watson & Sons Funeral Parlor in Texas ("Your loved one deserves the best"). Our client had sent the mortician's cars to the airport to pick us up. On the way, one of the musicians joked that we should play "Nearer My God to Thee," as though we were going to a New Orleans "second line" funeral. Another cartoon shows the hostess at one of our gigs pulling off a false finger to show me how it worked. She told me she had a wardrobe of prosthetic fingers, and each of them wore a different nail polish to match the color on the rest of her hands.

Roberta recorded an incident that took place at a fundraiser at the Four Seasons restaurant in New York, when I spotted a guest taking out his eye and cleaning it on the tablecloth. Another: I was playing at a wedding during Desert Storm, when a good friend who worked at the National Security Agency came over to apologize for being late. He explained that he'd been sending Tomahawk missiles to Baghdad. With that out of the way, he was ready to join the party. And another: a very small man with glasses and a bald head approached the piano. He was on a mission. He looked me over and in a deeply annoyed voice, said he thought Peter Duchin was dead. I told him *I* was Peter Duchin, assured him I was alive, and he scooted off, looking annoyed. Maybe he expected my father to be at the piano. The band thought that was hilarious.

Getting from one distant gig to another when they were booked a day or two apart was always a challenge. One time, when we had a job in Philadelphia, the only way to arrive on time was to fly to Washington, D.C., then drive up for a couple of hours. Not easy to arrange with a full band and instruments. We were able to avoid the extra leg of the trip because another passenger had a heart attack and the pilot had to make an emergency landing in . . . Philadelphia. I should have felt guilty that our good fortune was due to someone else's crisis, but I was just glad to avoid the long haul on the highway. I never found out if the other passenger survived.

That wasn't the only heart attack episode in my career. I hadn't been in the business for long when I was booked at the Fontainebleau hotel in Miami. I was playing at a tea dance, noticed a commotion, and saw that a man had collapsed on the dance floor. The maître d' rushed over and told me that under no circumstances—this definitely being a "circumstance"—was I to stop playing. The man was removed as quietly as possible; the hotel manager reminded me to keep the music going, and the dancers kept dancing.

Roberta's sense of humor has a way of perking up days when we're waiting around. At one job we were asked to play Andrews Sisters songs. That afternoon, Roberta took my eight musicians to a wig shop, bought period wigs for them, and one for me. Before the party started, I was onstage and she handed me a puffed-up, hair-sprayed blond wig. The Andrews Sisters had dark hair, but Roberta decided blond fit the image better. I put on the wig, but I didn't sing soprano, and I only kept it on long enough to give the band a laugh.

One of Roberta's cartoons reminded me of the New Year's Eve when we were hired for a terrific party in Miami, where the tables were placed around a pool. At midnight I started the countdown: "Five. Four . . ." stepped back to give the musicians the downbeat for "Auld Lang Syne," and fell into the pool, followed by several guests in full evening dress. The host loaned me a bathing suit, which I wore for the rest of the evening, playing with a towel around my shoulders.

After Roberta closed her cartoon notebook, the group promised to drop by another time, and left. The band was still being booked for jobs at which, of course, I wasn't featured, and I had a pang of longing when I watched them go. I didn't know whether we'd ever play together again.

P A R T   T W O

—

ABSENT
PRESENCES

"I was a son, parentless with what was not known
to a parentless son, and I could only step into frag-
ments of the story."

—Michael Ondaatje, *Warlight*

My library-cum-office became a temporary bedroom while
I recovered from my stroke. My bed faced a wall of bookcases
crowded with photographs of my parents: my mother, who died six
days after I was born; and my father, who died when I was twelve.
The images of a "family" that barely existed inspired me to explore
who Marjorie and Eddy Duchin really were.

CHAPTER SIX

Fragments

Playing the Blues

TWO MONTHS IN THE hospital, and finally home! Virginia and Adelle helped me into a cab, I breathed in the familiar New York air, tinted with the complex smell of the river, and I was ready to carry on. I was up to five out of ten on my physical ability test; I could speak pretty clearly; read more than a page without losing the plot; and get around with a walker. Although I could move my left hand, it didn't have any sensation, and if I tried to pick up a glass it would drop. I still had a lot of work to do.

As I left the hospital, I was reminded of a story I'd heard about Joan Rivers. It's said that a friend of hers had been released from a hospital on crutches, when Joan announced that she should throw away her crutches, scream "I've been saved," and walk away, as though she had been cured in Lourdes. I wasn't looking for a miracle, but I didn't expect the transition to leave me feeling flat and disoriented.

At the hospital, I knew what would happen, and when. The schedules were as reliable as they had been at boarding school; nurses and doctors were always around to check on me, and showed up more or less at the push of a buzzer. Even though dinner was brought in at the uncivilized hour of 4:30, I had learned to rely on the pattern. Back in our apartment, I didn't know what shape my days and nights would take. Being on my own was vertiginous.

It took me a few days before I was ready to try to play the reassuringly familiar baby grand Bechstein that had once belonged to my father. I went into the living room, using my walker, slid onto the bench, opened the lid, and looked at the clean black and white ivories. The first piece came naturally, an uncomplicated blues in F. My right hand worked as well as it had before the stroke; but once again, while the left automatically moved into position, it still just lay there. I sat with both hands on the piano and tried to *will* my hand to pick up the message from my brain, and I tried again.

This time, I chose the music for Bach's *Well-Tempered Clavier*. The first movement is relatively simple and slow, although Glenn Gould played it rather fast. Seeing the notes on paper required me to use both sides of my brain at the same time, but as any neurologist could have told me, that only made the situation worse.

I might have said "to hell with it" then, but my hand *had* improved. At least the fingers had begun to move. The only way to beat this damn thing was to keep trying. Practice! Practice! Practice!

Day after day, I returned to the piano, playing scales and doing exercises. The effort was agonizing. I began to hate that hand, as though it was purposely mocking me.

MY PICTURE GALLERY

VIRGINIA HAD MOVED A bed into my office-cum-library, where I would sleep while I was recovering. The bed (a

French antique with a padded headboard in a stylish but faded Provençal fabric) took up most of the room. My father's upholstered rocking chair was close by. The fabric is worn and ripped, but Dad had sat in it, and I couldn't part with it. I also have a pair of ivory-backed hairbrushes with his initials. I use them every day, even though it can feel a little strange to think that his hair was once in the same bristles.

The bed faces a run of bookcases so jammed that some of the volumes are stacked on their sides. When I first lay down, I tried to calculate how many steps I'd have to take from my bed to the bookcase wall. If I was on my way to the bathroom and felt wobbly, I wanted to know if I could make it that far and hold on until I regained my balance.

I'd been in that room countless times and gotten accustomed to its most obvious feature: the dozens of photographs of my parents, alone and together, propped against books and hung on the walls. I had surrounded myself with pictures of a mother I'd never known, and a father who was absent for most of my childhood. Now I felt as though I was seeing the images for the first time.

My Other Family

AMONG THE PHOTOGRAPHS, SMALLER, informal pictures showed Marie and Averell Harriman, who had offered to take care of me after my mother died.

I didn't live with them at first because I remained in the hospital for months. When I was finally released, I was equipped with oxygen tanks that kept me breathing until my lung was functioning properly. My doctor,

Averell and Marie, along with Dad and another of my mother's close friends, the author and screenwriter Anita Loos, decided I should live in a dry desert climate. Anita, known as "Neetsie" to me, who is most famous for writing *Gentlemen Prefer Blondes,* found a small house for my nurse Chissy and me in Palm Springs.

Chissy and I were transported to California in two private railroad cars, one for us and the other to carry the oxygen tanks. That was the kind of special treatment Averell could organize: his father, E. H. Harriman, had controlled the Union Pacific Railroad.

We stayed in Palm Springs for more than a year, mostly isolated, so I wouldn't be exposed to germs; although many Sundays, Neetsie drove three hours from Los Angeles to see me and Marie visited from time to time. I'm sure Chissy often picked me up, cuddled me, and did things I imagine a mother would have done, and I must have learned to walk and talk from her.

My lung healed, and I was installed at Arden, the Harrimans' twenty-thousand-acre estate with its one-hundred-room, forty-bedroom house. Arden was located in the New York town not coincidentally named Harriman. Averell's father, who bought the property and built the house, had needed an entire village—population 2,500—to accommodate the people who worked for him.

At Arden, Marie and Dad decided I should be taken care of by a governess, rather than a nurse. Chissy left, and a Frenchwoman named Zellie appeared. I felt adrift without Chissy, whom I adored and had relied on to take care of me and love me, but I came to love Zellie, too. She taught me to speak French, which came in handy later.

She also inadvertently showed me what a naked woman looked like when I walked into her room one morning without knocking, and found her standing on her head doing yoga, without a stitch on.

We lived in the big house until the Harrimans loaned it to the Navy as a rehabilitation center for returning veterans. Marie and her dachshunds, Mimi and the amusingly named Gary Cooper; Averell's Lab, Scotch; and Zellie and I moved down the hill into two white-painted cottages on the estate, one for Ave and Marie, whom I called "Ma," and the other for Zellie and me.

LICKING THE IVORIES

I WAS THREE YEARS old when Dad signed a six-month, multiyear contract to perform at the Waldorf. The first time I heard him play was the night he opened. My grandmother, who had been in mourning since my mother died, rarely went out, but she made an exception for Dad's debut, and brought me along. Dad was a great showman; his fingers rippled over the keyboard and he even had a mirror attached to the inside of the keyboard cover, so people could watch his hands. I was a bit confused: there was the Dad I sort of knew close up; and now I was seeing a kind of magician across the room. I understood that he was my father, but onstage he seemed like an enchanted stranger.

We had a piano in our cottage, which I wasn't supposed to touch, but I was fascinated by Dad's performance. When I was strong enough to open the lid, I furtively checked to see that no one was looking, gently stroked the keys, pounded on them, and listened. Then I bent over and licked the ivories. I wanted to know what they tasted like, not just how they sounded.

A Boy's Life

I BECAME PART OF the activities at Arden as soon as I could, tagging after Bill Kitchen, the property's caretaker. Bill was a wiry Scotsman with a prominent Adam's apple and a weathered face. He was sparing with his conversation, called Averell "The Governor," and in return was called "Kitchen." He encouraged me to hang around while he worked, and taught me simple tasks that made me feel quite useful. We planted a large Victory Garden, part of a nationwide war effort to encourage families to grow their own produce, so there would be more food for the fighting men. Bill also taught me to cast a plug with my small Ambassador reel in one of Arden's huge lakes, which were full of bass. When I was about ten, and he thought I was ready to handle a gun, he found a light .22 caliber rifle, and showed me how to shoot woodchucks. Averell, who had been a great polo player at Yale, had a stableful of fine horses, and forty miles of riding trails. The chucks dug large holes in the turf and a horse could break a leg by stepping in one. Bill drove me around in his Woody Pontiac, looking for the "culprits." When we shot one, we'd cut off its tail and put it in a barrel of salt to preserve it. Ave counted the tails and gave me a twenty-five-cent bounty for each one.

MY FATHER'S HAT

JIMMY STEWART, WHO HAD enlisted in the Air Force, was among Dad's friends who suggested that he join a fighting service, rather than spending the war entertaining the troops. Dad chose the Navy, was trained in Miami and Chicago, and sent overseas on a destroyer. He wrote unexpectedly affectionate letters on lightweight military paper from his ship; in one, he instructed Marie and Ave to arrange for me to take piano lessons. I did, but I much preferred to roam the woods, or go fishing. When Dad was on one of his rare leaves, he and a few friends came out to Arden. He would grab me in his arms and rub his rough cheeks against mine. I was overjoyed to see him, but I also felt sort of captive. It was a bit alarming.

The naval officers wore their uniforms, and when Dad picked me up, I carefully touched his medals and ribbons and epaulets. Sometimes he took off his hat and put it on my head. The cap almost covered my eyes, but I looked up from under the brim and asked if I could keep it. He said he needed it for work. Always, after a little while, he left.

I've heard that Dad told people one of the reasons he chose to fight was to make his son proud, but that I never asked him to tell me war stories. I did know one. As a musician with perfect pitch, he was in charge of the sonar on his ship. He was on duty one night when he heard some odd signals and thought he'd identified a submarine. He ordered the crew to drop depth charges, and a whale floated to the surface. The guys on board never let him forget it.

My father had a distinguished naval career, serving as

a combat officer on destroyer squadrons during Operation Overlord at Normandy, and at Iwo Jima and Okinawa. He left the Navy with the rank of lieutenant commander, and won seven medals for his courage during dangerous engagements. I might have thought of him as a hero, but all I really cared about was that he was away.

Averell and Marie weren't around much either. In the 1930s, Marie had her own art gallery; and during the war she worked for the USO and stayed at their house in Manhattan most weekdays. Ave, who was one of FDR's most trusted and effective diplomats, worked on Lend-Lease in London before the U.S. entered the war; then served as the American ambassador to the Soviet Union from 1943 to 1946.

He had seen a newsreel of the Red Square victory parade when he was there, and mentioned how much he admired the Russian cavalry horses. At the end of the war, I was at Arden when two thoroughbreds arrived, a gift from Stalin for Ave and his daughter Kathleen, a brilliant rider who had accompanied him to the Soviet Union. The horses were attended by a vet, a jockey, two grooms, and documentation bound in red leather. Ave had given me a pony for my third birthday and I had proudly graduated to a small horse when the Russian steeds arrived. They stood about sixteen hands high. It was quite a while before I was allowed to ride the stallion.

Nearly all the children I met went to the local public school in the village. I didn't get to play with them, or even know them very well, because when the school day was over, I was collected and transported back up the hill. I could have been lonely, but up at Arden there was plenty to do, and I had Zellie and Bill. I often wondered about my mother and missed the idea of her, and I wished my Dad could come ashore to see me more often, but I accepted what I had and made the best of it. I didn't know anything else.

Over the years, that acceptance was mixed with grief, loneliness, and sometimes anger. When I became a father, I knew that, as much as I traveled for work, I would never have left my children to grow up essentially on their own. The more I looked at the pictures of my parents, the more I wanted to understand who they were, not only in relation to me, but as themselves.

IMPRESSIONS

MANY OF THE IMAGES in my room were dramatic studio shots taken by my mother's close friend, the writer, artist, and photographer Cecil Beaton. Most were of my mother, but some were of Dad, or of the two of them together. A bunch of pictures of my father weren't quite posed, but they weren't really casual either, often showing him with other entertainers, who were among his friends: Bing Crosby, with whom he had a radio show; Nat King Cole; Ethel Merman; and Count Basie.

Even my hero, Joe DiMaggio, was in one of the pictures, standing by the piano, appearing to sing while my father played. Joe was far more than a great baseball player; he was a symbol of the way most Americans liked to think of themselves: decent, unaffected, self-made, with a shared sense of patriotism.

He had been featured in a number of songs. The

first, "Joltin' Joe DiMaggio," was released on November 10, 1941, in honor of the U.S. Marine Corps' birthday. Pearl Harbor was almost exactly a month later; war was on everyone's mind, and the refrain was "Joe, Joe DiMaggio / We want you on our side." It reached number sixteen on the music charts.

In 1967, during the national upheaval over the Vietnam War, Paul Simon wrote the music and lyrics for the song "Mrs. Robinson," which was featured in the 1968 movie *The Graduate*. The plaintive refrain in the title song, "Where have you gone, Joe DiMaggio?/Our nation turns its lonely eyes to you," once again has a frightening resonance.

When Joe heard the lyrics, he was irritated. One night, he and Paul Simon were in the same restaurant and Paul went over and introduced himself. He told him, " 'I'm the guy that wrote "Mrs. Robinson," ' and he said 'Yeah, sit down . . . why'd you say that? I'm here, everyone knows I'm here.' I said, 'I don't mean it that way—I mean, where are these great heroes now?' He was flattered once he understood."

In college, and as I moved from one apartment or house to another, I brought the pictures with me and placed them where I could look at them. I might have unconsciously arranged them to create the illusion that I was part of a family; but sometimes they had the opposite effect. There were no photographs of me alone, or at the piano playing a gig. Where was I?

I do have one picture that gives a family-like impression. Marie, my father, and I were in Sands Point, Long Island, where the Harrimans had a summer house. I must have been about three or four years old, sun-browned and wearing a freshly ironed white playsuit. I remember clothes like that, worn by children who lived in households with full-time laundresses.

Crouched down between the grown-ups, I'm inspecting something Dad is holding in his open palm. He is squatting, looking at me and grinning. Marie is perched on a rock, gazing at him. Dad was dressed in a suit, so he must only have been there for the day. He probably had to get back to the city for a gig that night. I don't know who took the picture, maybe my governess Zellie. That picture is in a silver frame with the initials E.D. at the top.

Ave was in London at the time, and gossip columnists noted that my father was Marie's regular "escort." I once asked her if they had had an affair. "None of your damn business," she said. Then she admitted that she had been in love with him, but couldn't imagine being a bandleader's wife.

I wonder which of us Dad had come to see that day.

While I rested, facing the photographs, I began to look at them from a new perspective. It was time to pull myself together and integrate what was real with the feelings I had been trying to push away all my life.

My mother was a close friend of the superb photographer, artist, and writer Cecil Beaton, who loved to photograph her. I've always wished the woman in this picture could stand up, stretch, show me her wonderful smile and put her arms around me.

Photograph by Cecil Beaton

CHAPTER SEVEN

The Mystery
of Marjorie

If We Passed on the Street

MY FATHER WASN'T AROUND much, but at least I knew him and I was always thrilled to see him. I have a trove of memories, information, and publicity "facts" about him. But I knew almost nothing about my mother. Her friends described her as beautiful, funny, and adventuresome. They also told me that her nickname was "Bubbles," which sounds pretty silly. That was it.

The photographs of her are of a woman younger than my daughter, Courtnay, is now. My father was half my current age. Together, they look glamorous and deeply in love, but I had been seeing them in two dimensions, permanently fixed in black and white on paper. I wanted to add depth to the pictures and learn what my parents were like when they were young, before my birth killed my mother, and changed my father. Sometimes, I still secretly blame myself for her death, and for Dad's absence during my childhood.

For eight decades, I only had one picture of my mother with me. She is half-asleep in Manhattan's Harbor Sanitarium, where I was born, holding me against her cheek. I can only see a glimpse of my head, but I'm there, in her arms. My father is kneeling by the bed with an expression of pure joy. My grandmother looms behind him, a large woman wearing a stylish hat and a dress with an enormous white collar. My godmother, Ginny Chambers, is just visible in the background.

Searching in newspaper archives, I was astonished to find a far better photograph, which illustrates an article rather gruesomely titled "Motherhood Ends Life of Mrs. Duchin."

The image is blurry, but I can see my mother's face, with what I once read that *Vogue* described as her "butterfly eyebrows," and her sleepy, contented expression. She is holding a bottle; I am sucking the milk with pursed lips, and I already have a thatch of the black hair that mostly stayed that color until I had my stroke.

I can't imagine why a newspaper photographer was allowed into the room to photograph a new mother and her infant, but I'm glad he, or maybe she, was there.

The Harbor Sanitarium (note that it was not called the Harbor *Hospital*) accommodated privileged New Yorkers who wanted privacy, luxury, and hotel services. Society's favorite restaurant, the Colony—where patrons could leave their dogs with Clara, the ladies' room attendant, while they enjoyed their meals—was on the first floor; and patients often ordered meals from downstairs to be delivered to their rooms. My mother had lunch there the day she went into labor. One of her friends recalled that she said she didn't know why she had decided to have her baby at a fashionable sanitarium, instead of a better-equipped hospital. The women assured her that everything would be fine, and that it was a *very* pleasant place to recover. Harbor was popular for plastic surgery, minor operations, or for those who wanted to enjoy the two-week postpartum period that was usual in those days, while they turned their babies over to a nurse. It did not attract a first-rate medical team. After I was delivered, my mother's doctor left for a two-week fishing trip. The physician who was covering for him said he didn't want to take over a colleague's patient.

There was every reason to assume that we would go home as soon as we were ready. Instead, my mother developed peritonitis, suffered a fatal hemorrhage, and died six days later. My grandmother was so distraught the doctors gave her a room until she felt well enough to leave. The Harbor Sanitarium closed not long after my mother's highly publicized death.

I will never know what Marjorie Oelrichs Duchin would have been like if she had lived, or what kind of mother she would have been. She simply stops in the pictures, while she continues in one scene after another in my mind. Would we recognize each other if we passed on the street? Of course not. I owed it to myself and to her to try to find out more.

I Begin My Search

MY MOTHER WAS EIGHT years old when Marjorie Sr. divorced my grandfather Charles de Loosey Oelrichs. My grandmother filed for divorce in Paris, where, according to one newspaper report, she discreetly "Declined to make known the charges or other circumstances leading to the divorce decree."

Charles, who worked for his family's Hamburg-based shipping company, was either unable or unwilling to support his former wife and their only child. That shouldn't have been a problem. His great-uncle, Hermann Oelrichs, had been married to Teresa ("Tessie") Fair. Tessie and her sister Virginia, known as "Birdie," who married William K. Vanderbilt, were two of the richest women in the United States. They had each inherited $20 million (worth more than $500 million today) from their father, James Graham Fair, an Irish immigrant miner who was among four partners who discovered the Comstock Lode, the largest deposit of silver ever found. By the time the mine had been pretty much tapped out, it had netted $300 million (worth about $6 billion today). Tessie was so rich she could never spend her money in her lifetime, although she gave it a damn good try.

When her husband, Hermann, died in 1906, he left everything to his brother, my great-grandfather Charles May Oelrichs. Charles and his wife, Blanche, lived in Newport and New York, where they entertained extravagantly, which is saying a lot in the Gilded Age. Their son, my grandfather, also named Charles, inherited a comfortable fortune, but he followed his parents' example and spent profligately. By the time he and my grandmother were married, they lived relatively modestly. I once visited the house in Newport where my mother spent the summers: it was quite nice, but it certainly was not a mansion.

After the divorce, the two Marjories were left financially adrift, but my grandmother was undaunted. According to an article in Wisconsin's *Eau Claire Leader,* Marjorie Sr., who was "noted for her unique gowns and for her initiative, recently attracted considerable attention by engaging in business." It might seem surprising that she was the subject of an item in a small-town Midwestern paper, but readers all over the United States were fascinated by New York, Newport, and Palm Beach society. Even *The New York Times* published front-page stories about their lavish parties.

Around the time my grandparents divorced, my grandmother discovered a unique French perfume and became its sole source in the United States. In 1921, she opened a boutique on Madison Avenue, selling the perfume and assorted bibelots. Five years later, the *Chicago Tribune* featured a photograph of her in her shop. She had a soft, pretty face, was posed with one hand on her hip, and wore a stylish coat with a huge faux flower at the neck, and a wide band of fur at the hem. My mother was eighteen by then, already making her mark among her contemporaries, but Marjorie Sr. doesn't look much older than thirty.

The caption under the photograph reads:

> BETWEEN SOCIETY AND SHOP alternates the life of Mrs. Marjorie Oelrichs. Five years ago, she began her business venture in New York after divorcing Charles de Loosey Oelrichs, a New York society man, in Paris. In the years that had elapsed she has met increasing success, and at the same time found leisure for the social whirl.

My grandmother opened a second shop on Bellevue Avenue in Newport, and in 1927 she wrote a book, titled *Home Beauty Course.* The first chapter begins "You are a type—envy no other." It appears that my mother took that advice.

The perfume became such an integral part of my grandmother's identity that she liberally doused herself in the scent. Of course, I never knew the slim, stylish woman who was photographed in 1926; I only remember the grandmother who hugged me against her commodious bosom. The sweet odor was a little off-putting.

Alexander Woollcott, the pudgy, brilliant, and acerbic *New Yorker* writer, famed for such quips as "All the things I really like to do are either illegal, immoral or fattening," gave me a rather different view. Anita Loos quotes him as writing that my mother "was trailed by her mother, known as Big Marge, soft, plump and beautiful, who was a high society version of [the actress] Mae West. Her voice was a sort of sexy wheeze, but contrary to Mae, her brain was like a bag of popcorn." I'd like to think he meant that she was full of ideas, but I'm afraid that wasn't his intention.

I only met my grandfather Charles a couple of times. In my late teens, I went to see him at his house in a pleasant quasi-suburban neighborhood in Forest Hills, Queens. He was wearing a well-cut but shabby suit, and had a white beard and white hair that needed a barber's attention. He was married to his third wife, whom I heard he had met when she was working as a waitress at a nearby Schrafft's restaurant. Schrafft's was a modestly priced New York–based chain, which served the kind of "nursery food" Andy Warhol once said he craved. (Andy had declared, perhaps to shock, that he would like to open a similar restaurant, but his would feature waitresses dressed in nursemaids' uniforms.)

My grandfather didn't ask me about school or my life,

and our conversation was short and stilted. I told him I would come to see him again, but I never did.

THE AUNTS

IT WAS EASIER TO understand my mother when I learned that my grandmother was just one of her three unconventional role models.

My grandmother's sister, Alice Turnbull Hopkins, was a famous suffragist, who campaigned against Woodrow Wilson because he was opposed to allowing women the vote. During his 1917 campaign, she drove through Illinois with a banner that read "Don't Vote for Wilson." When he was elected, she picketed the White House with other suffragists dressed in white, and was arrested and sentenced to serve time in the Occoquan Workhouse. She was released after three days, but even a short stint in jail was a badge of honor in the movement. She left proudly wearing her prison uniform, so newspaper photographers could take her picture.

Women won the vote, and Alice announced that she was a socialist and lectured widely. In her next phase, she opened a dress shop called Marjane. She and my grandmother were Turnbulls, an old, respected New York family; maybe her society friends ignored her politics and bought her clothes.

And then there was my mother's exotic paternal aunt, Charles's sister, Blanche Oelrichs the famous poet, author, and playwright, who wrote under the byline Michael Strange. The French portrait painter Paul Helleu described her as "the most beautiful woman in America." I've seen her picture and she was a great beauty, but she was more interested in living the life she chose than relying on her looks. Her writing was heavily influenced by Walt Whitman, but unfortunately not enough.

Blanche had three husbands, most famously the actor John Barrymore, whom she married in 1920, immediately after he was released from an institution where he had been treated for a nervous breakdown. They divorced five years later, but they had a passionate relationship while it lasted. In one of his prolific letters to her (he calls her "Fig"—I don't think I want to know why) he wrote: "Baby, my treacle, my own sweet love / He [referring to himself] is writing in his own men place and [wishes?] most terribly for his Fig . . . baby, I get choked up with gusts of loneliness for my own sweet mother, my baby, my thing . . ." and on it goes. Despite his apparent obsession with Blanche, their daughter, my cousin Diana Barrymore, wrote that when her father visited her at boarding school, he tried to seduce one of her friends in the backseat of his limousine.

Blanche's last husband was Harrison Tweed, a prominent lawyer, chairman of the board of Sarah Lawrence College, and briefly its acting president. When Blanche divorced him, she lived in an intimate relationship with Margaret Wise Brown, another socialite gone rogue. Brown, who wrote the still beloved children's books *The Runaway Bunny* and *Goodnight Moon,* celebrated her first royalty payment by purchasing a cartful of flowers to decorate her apartment. Sadly, I never met her, although I've read some of her books. Blanche died in 1950; Margaret died two years later.

LUCKY STRIKES, POND'S COLD CREAM, AND CECIL BEATON

MARJORIE SR. COULD AFFORD to pay for her daughter's debut, but after that my mother had to support herself. She began by modeling, endorsing commercial products. Edward Steichen photographed her for Pond's Cold Cream ads that appeared in *Ladies' Home Journal*. A 1926 article in the Washington, D.C., *Evening Star* features a picture of her, over the title "Miss Marjorie Oelrichs Speaks to New York's Brilliant Younger Set." She is described as warning, "The hectic whirl of dances, formal functions, and sports, conspire to ruin the most velvety skin! And they would—but for Pond's Two Creams, which come to the rescue. So says Miss Marjorie Oelrichs, now in her second year in the brilliant life of New York's young set."

Marjorie wasn't the only Society woman to lend or sell her name commercially, imbuing everyday products with the illusion of exclusivity. Pond's also signed up Mrs. Oliver Harriman and Mrs. August Belmont: in that era, with few exceptions, a woman was listed by her husband's name. President Theodore Roosevelt's ungovernable daughter, Alice Longworth, who also modeled to promote products, ignored that as she did most other rules.

Marjorie also appeared in Lucky Strike ads, again photographed by Steichen. My son Colin found a poster of her in a Lucky's ad on eBay, and it now hangs in my room. I was in prep school when a friend took a picture of me holding a sign that read "Be Happy—Go Lucky!" with an image of a cigarette pack and the motto "Luckies Taste Better." The brand had found a loyal market.

My mother also occasionally wrote magazine articles. She was eighteen when her story "What's the Matter with American Men?" was published in *Liberty* magazine. Foreign men, she explained, "have learned that love is among the fine arts. . . . A European man is a gallant lover." The piece ended on a conciliatory note: "I have told only why I prefer foreign men to American men. I do not say I expect to marry a foreigner." (She came close by marrying the son of immigrants.) The story was considered risqué enough that it was often mentioned in her profiles.

In 1929 CBS Radio hired her as its fashion director, with a 10:30 p.m. slot. The series opened with "Part I of a biographical radio narrative, 'Marjorie Oelrichs tells a story.'" I couldn't discover what else was included in the nineteen-year-old's series, or if it even continued. I guess it was more of the usual "High Society" chatter.

Like me, my mother lived in Paris for a while, more or less supporting herself by finding apartments for rich Americans to rent. I wonder if she stayed with Ginny and Brose Chambers, as I would twenty years later, at the beginning of my junior year abroad, until I moved to the barge. Ginny was likely to have recommended Marjorie to potential real estate clients, maybe at one of the salons she held in that beautiful house. The entrance was a marvelous surprise: behind a high wall, a grove of orange trees led to a Tudor-style half-timbered building.

At the Chamberses', I met people who had known my mother: artists; the very rich, among them various Rothschilds; Cecil Beaton; and the art historian John Richardson, who would become a good friend, but I didn't learn a lot about her from them. Some would say, "Oh,

you're Marjorie's boy," and then the same old adjectives—
"beautiful," "funny," "adventurous," and so on—with the
inevitable follow-up: "Do you play the piano, like your
father?" One day, Mary Martin came to lunch. She told
me she was delighted to meet me, and explained that my
father had accompanied her on her first hit record, "My
Heart Belongs to Daddy." That was a fantastic piece of
information, and I was quite excited. She asked if I happened to know the song. I said "Sure," wandered over to
the piano and played, while she sat next to me on the
bench and sang. That was a real thrill.

I was back at Yale for my senior year when Mary was
doing a television show and asked me to play the song
with her. It would have been a great opportunity, but the
Harrimans and Chiquita thought it was too early for me
to perform in public, that it would go to my head, and I
needed to finish my studies.

Years later, when I was playing at the Maisonette,
Mary came in for dinner with her son, Larry Hagman,
who had become a pal of mine, and said, "Do you think
they would let you do it now?"

Jazz clubs were another aspect of my mother's Paris
world. Long after she died, Bricktop, the singer and performer, who owned the famous Parisian jazz club Chez
Bricktop, sent me a photograph of Marjorie wearing a
softly draped floor-length black dress, standing with her
arm around her friend, the singer Mabel Mercer. Bricktop,
whose real name was Ada Beatrice Queen Victoria Louise
Virginia Smith, was a cigar-smoking African American
with freckles and reddish hair, which accounted for her

nickname. In the 1920s, Cole Porter hired her for parties to show guests how to dance the Charleston and the unfortunately named Black Bottom. Porter later wrote "Miss Otis Regrets" for her to perform.

In Paris, when I went out for an evening of jazz, I sometimes felt that my mother's shadow was accompanying me. I hoped it was.

Marjorie became one of Cecil Beaton's favorite subjects and most intimate friends, intimate enough that he wrote in his diary, "When I had confided to her my lack of sex life & that I had never been to bed with a woman, she volunteered her services in my first experiment—& if this sounds comic, it was done from the best motives." I never met him, and I'll never know if he accepted her offer.

Beaton's portrait of the woman I would most like to have known shows Marjorie in a pose so natural that it looks as though he had just caught her in a perfect moment. She is resting her chin on her lightly clasped hands, leaning on what looks like a pillow loosely covered with fish netting. Her wavy blond hair is soft and unfussy; she's wearing a couple of big rings, a chunky beaded bangle bracelet, and a sweater: chic and simple. What makes the picture sing is her big open smile, her bright eyes, and her projection of calm happiness. For all her international experience, as Beaton would later write, she looks like "the best kind of American girl." I desperately want her to stand up and stretch, then put her arms around me. That's probably my favorite image of her; Marie must have felt the same way, because she had the same photograph on her bureau.

I'm lucky to have those images, but what I miss are the pictures that *aren't* there, the ones neither Beaton nor anyone else would ever be able to take.

My mother continued to work: she studied art and was hired to paint murals for her friends. I saw one on the walls of an indoor tennis court on Long Island, but I was there so long ago that, to my frustration, I can't bring up an image of what it looked like. Her most successful enterprise was as an interior decorator. I've seen a couple of pictures of her work: a Palm Beach dining room with bamboo-paneled walls, and a sleek Art Deco living room in a ski lodge, chic, simple, and modern, just like Marjorie. One long-lived example of her style is the Lodge at Averell's new resort in Sun Valley, Idaho. The year before I was born, Marie and my mother went to work: Ave wanted to build the exterior out of logs, but Marjorie warned him they would eventually rot and have to be replaced. She suggested that he have molds made of real logs, fill them with concrete, and assured him that they would look authentic, and would last.

Her special project was the bar, where she used a striking combination of blue and orange. She also designed the furniture for some of the bedrooms. Ave liked the look of the bar so much that he called it the Duchin Room. Guests were surprised to discover that my mother, not my father, was the inspiration. Fifty years later, I played at the Lodge, to celebrate Sun Valley's half-century anniversary. The concrete logs were holding up, as they are today, and the bar was still named for my mother.

"A BEAUTIFUL FRIENDSHIP"

MARJORIE WAS A REGULAR at the famously fabulous Central Park Casino. Dad and his band were the stars, but on opening night 1934, she was the main attraction. The New York *Daily News* gave her a front-page headline: "Young Marjorie Oelrichs Just Swirling in Eddies." The other "Eddie" in question was a chain store heir, described as Palm Beach's "chief beau" of the season. The *Daily News* wrote: "The jovial (and shall we say plump) Eddie gave Marjorie a terrific rush . . . while Marjorie was the guest, first of Mrs. Graham Fair Vanderbilt and then of Princess Ilynski and her husband, the Grand Duke Dmitri."

Under the subhead "But Is It Merely a Beautiful Friendship?" the story reads, "It's an interesting coincidence . . . that Marjorie staged the fashion show last night which was a feature of the Fall opening of the Central Park Casino. The Casino wouldn't be home if the darkly handsome Eddie [*sic*] and his orchestra weren't there to make music for dancing."

A year later, my parents were married in my grandmother's apartment at the Hotel Pierre. The room was decorated with a profusion of white flowers, but Marjorie disdained to be married in white: she wore what the newspapers described as "an afternoon gown of flowered taffeta, with a small black hat and carried a bouquet of gardenias." I was surprised to read that she was "given in marriage by her father." I had assumed he had drifted out of my mother's life after he and my grandmother were divorced and he remarried. The wedding was performed by a judge, in front of a small group of friends.

A photograph that was published in newspapers all over the country shows the newly married couple standing close together, arms linked, with Dad's hand resting on my mother's wrist. The "small black hat" was, in fact, quite large and tilted at an angle. Eddy was dressed in a wide-lapeled pinstriped suit with a white carnation in his lapel. He looked handsome, young, and slightly stunned. My mother was twenty-six (or as some reports claimed, twenty-seven). Dad was a year younger. They would only have two years together before Marjorie died.

Their marriage gave the gossip columnists plenty to write about. The *Daily News* cattily noted that my grandmother was "going to have something of a social problem on her own hands when her new son-in-law Eddy Duchin, the jazz orchestra leader, arrives on Bailey's sands with his new wife." In those days, Newport's exclusive Bailey's Beach club didn't accept Jews as members, and probably not as guests.

I've always declined jobs at "restricted" clubs or resorts, not because of Dad, or because I'm half-Jewish, but because I despise bigotry. Most clubs have changed their membership policies, if modestly, in the past couple of decades, but some manage to cling to their retrograde rules. A couple of years after my stroke, when I was working again, I was asked to play for a big party at a well-known restricted club in a winter resort. It would have been a good gig, but I turned the job down.

A Postcard and a Diary

NEARLY A CENTURY AFTER my mother wrote an ordinary "wish-you-were-here"-type postcard to Anita Loos, I was looking for mentions of her online and accidentally discovered a rare-documents site with a postcard from Marjorie Oelrichs. I can't imagine why someone saved a card from a nearly forgotten Society woman, but there it was. It is the only example of my mother's handwriting I have ever seen. The card cost $240 and I bought it.

Marjorie was in Austria, skiing with a beau, Count Felix Schaffgotsch. The count (who later, but probably not *much* later, given the trajectory of events, became a fervent Nazi) was a friend of Ave's, and helped persuade him to establish Sun Valley.

Looking for a fresh outlook on my mother, I called Renata Propper, an experienced graphologist, who is regularly hired by big corporations to provide insight about senior executives they are considering hiring. She reported:

> Marjorie not only was special, she wanted to be perceived as special. Even within the small framework of this postcard, she projects a strong, seductive vitality, exuberance and love of life.
>
> Her handwriting indicates a conventional upper-class upbringing . . . however she did not quite fit this mold, bursting out and beyond limiting rules and conventional behavior. . . . It seems that her . . . bravado camouflaged a more vulnerable precariously balanced core. . . . She liked to

shock, using her lively charm and strong will . . . with an invisible motto: "I can do this, too . . ."

As a mother she probably would have been sometimes overwhelmingly loving and charming, but other times somewhat elusive. . . . From a child's perspective, she might have been "a shining star on an imaginary firmament."

Renata had never met my mother; she lived in Austria until 1958, hadn't heard of Marjorie until I contacted her, and the usual internet search engines barely mentioned her. Pretty much all she knew was that my mother died almost immediately after I was born. She used her instincts and training to provide the rest.

Her conclusions have much in common with Cecil Beaton's diary description. Beaton was visiting a friend in Capri; they had finished lunch, and his hostess began to slit open the envelopes in a stack of letters, and read the letters aloud. One contained a clipping. "Hullo," she said, "What's this?"—"Mrs. Marjorie Oelrichs Duchin, wife of Eddy Duchin, pianist, after the birth of a son, DIED!" (Emphasis Beaton's.) That evening, he wrote his version of my mother's "obituary" in his diary:

It is as if all trees had died, all skies, all fruit, all music—so essential a part of existence was Marjorie. One couldn't think of her as being ill. . . . She was so healthy & serene & big & alive & though often depressed & things went wrong, she seemed so infinitely capable of looking after life.

She had a hard life with her mother's extrava-

gance, her own extravagance & unending finan-
cial difficulties. She had worked to make money.
She had been in states of indecision lasting years
about her affairs, her beaux, her interests, & at
last all had seemed smoothed out serenely. She
had been bold enough to marry the Pianist Eddy
Duchin . . . he turned out to be everything she
had hoped him to be and everybody else adored
him. . . . Marjorie was one of my best friends in
the most serious sense of the word. . . . She would
criticize me when I behaved poorly. She would
say, "Now really!" But she could be relied upon
to be devoted and her feelings were very deep
{and} with her, there were more laughs than with
anyone. . . . For her integrity, loyalty, courage and
sensibility, she was the best American girl I have
known. . . . She was incapable of snobbery and
sham. . . . [When] she came to tea and took off
her shoes and twiddled her big ring around her
little finger & smoked too many cigarettes and
combed her long pageboy's hair & flung back her
head & with a sweet smile that was almost a sneer
would say in a dry, crackly voice, "What's noo?" I
am haunted by her smile.

I am equally haunted by a comment Beaton wrote
that she had made when she was pregnant with me: "She
had giggled and said, 'Well you know I'm not really
the mother type, but you know a girl must go through
with this sort of thing and it'll be fun and it'll be all
right.'"

Nearly Touching

I WAS ENTERING FIFTH grade when I was sent to Eagle-brook, a pre-prep boys' boarding school. In those more spartan postwar days, we never had enough heat, and we slept in one big barracks-like room with partitions between the beds. Some nights, I could hear my home-sick classmates trying to muffle their tears after lights-out. I had lived in a few places by then, so getting used to Eaglebrook wasn't as hard for me as it was for some of the other boys. The aspect of life at boarding school that most surprised me was how easy it was to fit in, as long as I followed the rules.

That year, the boys were obsessed with Erskine Caldwell's 1933 novel, *God's Little Acre,* and at night, many of them read it with a flashlight under the covers. The book was so filled with sex that the New York Society for the Suppression of Vice petitioned a state court to censor it. They failed: the book sold more than 10 million copies, with an Armed Services edition during World War II.

If my mother had lived, I might have gone to a day school in New York, like so many of the boys I knew, and only left for boarding school in the ninth grade. Home would have been the apartment at 2 East 60th Street, which she had just finished decorating, with a room for the baby. I like to think my friends would have wanted to hang out there after school because she was fun to be around, unlike other Society women who greeted their children's friends more formally, then went back to their adult lives.

My imagination sticks when I get to my graduation

from college. I can't think of Marjorie as a middle-aged woman or a grandmother. I can only see her as she was in the pictures in my room.

I don't usually remember my dreams, but not long after my stroke, I woke up with the distinct feeling that my mother was near me. I dreamt that we were scuba diving together in clear blue Caribbean water, swimming so close we were nearly touching. I was having a wonderful time, when the water suddenly turned dark, and I couldn't see her anymore.

"A fine romance . . ." The newspapers feasted on the love story
between the socialite and the bandleader. Cecil Beaton beautifully
captured the happiness, intimacy, and glamour that was abruptly
cut off when my mother died.

Photograph by Cecil Beaton

CHAPTER EIGHT

Eddy, Here and Then Gone

A Different View

MY FEELINGS ABOUT MY father have always been complicated, but after my stroke I developed more empathy for him: I, too, know what it feels like to fight an illness with all the strength one can muster, and how depressing it is to have to deal with mortality for the first time. Dad was forty, at the top of his career after twenty years in the business he loved, when he contracted leukemia, a malignant cancer of the blood. In the 1950s, one of the few treatments for the disease was cortisone, which made his face swell up grotesquely. He tried to act as though he'd be fine, but he didn't look like the Dad I knew. I understood he was seriously ill, but I had no idea that he was going to die, or that this time he would be gone for good. When I was still a child, after he died, sometimes when I was in a car at night, I tried to stay awake, in case he suddenly, inexplicably, appeared by the side of the road, waiting to meet me.

Instead of remembering Eddy mostly as a father who popped in and out of my life, I tried to reframe my view, to consider the kind of man he was, and not just in terms of our shared musical ability.

His photographs didn't help much. He's smiling in nearly every one, as though he is always conscious that someone is looking at him, or taking his picture. If you didn't know any better, you'd think he was perennially happy. His smile was sometimes known as "the Ipana smile," after a popular toothpaste of the day. Who knows, maybe he had a deal with the company.

THE MUSIC GENE

I ALWAYS ASSUMED THAT Dad and I were the only professional musicians in the Duchin line, but it turns out that music was in our makeup, at least from the late nineteenth century, and maybe earlier. My father's parents, Frank and Tillie Duchin, were immigrants from Kiev, where my paternal great-grandmother was a piano teacher. Her daughter, my grandmother Tillie, loved music and the radio was on all day. Dad grew up hearing symphonies, operas, and Big Bands. He took lessons in classical music, but the popular bands had their own attraction. When he played professionally, he would use his classical technique to create his own dramatic and romantic style for dancing.

By the late 1880s, Frank and Tillie had settled in Cambridge, Massachusetts, where Frank, who was one of eleven children, followed at least two of his brothers. The family name in Russia was Duchinsky, but one brother who preceded Frank and Tillie had "Americanized" his name to Dickson. Maybe my grandfather thought that was too different from the original; it certainly didn't sound Jewish, and Frank just dropped the "sky." I've heard that the different names led to a permanent rift. Whatever the reason, the brothers remained estranged.

Dad was born in 1910, the elder of two children; the

other was my Aunt Lil, whom I knew and liked a lot. There's no evidence that Lil was musical, but Eddy started taking piano lessons from a local teacher at the age of seven. He was thirteen when his teacher recommended that he work with the more advanced Felix Fox in Boston. Twice a week, Tillie accompanied him to his lessons on the streetcar, a trip that took an hour each way. She was determined that her son have every chance to become as good a pianist as he could be.

Frank was a tailor. He made uniforms for firemen and policemen, as well as other clients. When my father had his band, if he had a gig in Boston and one of the musicians needed his tuxedo fixed, Frank would do the job, and have it back to him the same day. He was successful enough that he was able to give his son a baby grand piano for his sixteenth birthday.

In his teens, Dad was hired to play at local bar mitzvahs. As soon as he had accumulated the cash, he bought himself a Peerless sedan. I have a picture of him posing in front of a snappy-looking convertible, but it was taken in 1935, when he could afford the more luxurious Hudson Terraplane. (The Terraplane slogan was "On the sea that's aquaplaning, in the air that's aeroplaning, but on the land, in the traffic, on the hills, hot diggity dog, THAT'S TERRAPLANING.")

COUSIN HARRY

THE DUCHINS AND THE Dicksons lived in the same town, yet I was barely aware that Dad's first cousin, Harry Ellis Dickson, who was two years older, was also a musical prodigy: he began violin lessons when he was six. Harry studied at the New England Conservatory and the Hochschule für Musik in Berlin. When he returned to the U.S., Serge Koussevitzky hired him to play in the violin section of the Boston Symphony Orchestra. Harry was short, wore glasses, and had a pleasant, but not memorable face, the physical opposite of my father. He was a highly accomplished musician, but without Dad's looks and personality, he was unlikely to have become a popular star.

He became the concertmaster of the BSO instead, and he and Arthur Fiedler worked to make it one of the best orchestras in the country. According to Harry's April 2, 2003, obituary—he died at the age of ninety-four—he served under five music directors. In 1959 he founded the BSO's youth concert series, and in his "retirement" he was the music director of the Boston Classical Orchestra.

While Harry was busy building up the BSO, Dad had become known as "The Magic Fingers of the Piano." He even insured his hands for $150,000 (nearly $2.6 million today). I wish I'd had the foresight to take out that kind of insurance.

Boston named a park after Harry, and the French government awarded him the title of chevalier of arts and letters. Sadly, Dad's best-known "monument" was the film that bears his name.

A PHARMACIST MANQUÉ

FRANK AND TILLIE WORRIED that their son wouldn't be able to support himself as a musician, and insisted that he go to pharmacy school. Years later, I met Edward Breck, who founded Breck & Company, which produced the nationally known shampoo. He told me he remembered Dad from pharmacy college, but to my disappointment he wasn't able to give me any details about what he was like at that age. What he wasn't, however, was a pharmacist. As soon as he graduated, he set off for New York, with the bold innocence of youth and the brazen belief that he could make it as a pianist and bandleader.

Dad had so little money that he couldn't afford to rent even a single room in New York, and when he met Sonny Werblin, a fledgling agent at MCA, they decided to share an apartment. Cash was so short that they had to take turns having their shirts laundered.

Sonny Werblin was a great talent-spotter and promoter. He recognized a future star, and I believe Dad was one of the first big acts he represented. Sonny became a hugely powerful agent at MCA; his clients included the most important people in entertainment and sports. One of his greatest coups was to get football on television. He and a partner, Leon Hess of Hess Oil, bought the New York Jets and drafted Joe Namath.

I often sat in Sonny's box at Shea Stadium, and thought about what a great time he and Dad would have had together. Sonny was also the president of Madison Square Garden; thanks to him, I took my kids to hockey games there. My daughter, Courtnay, had a crush on one of the hockey players, and Sonny gave her one of his jerseys for Christmas. I'm not sure she ever washed it.

"The Night Spot That Roared"

DAD WAS EIGHTEEN WHEN he was booked for his first gig, at the Ross Fenton Farm, an attractive summer nightclub overlooking the sea in Asbury Park, New Jersey. When the season was over, he landed an audition with Leo Reisman, one of New York's top bandleaders, whose band was playing at the Waldorf. I'm sure Reisman thought he was about to waste his time auditioning a good-looking kid with unrealistic ambitions. Then Eddy placed his hands on the keys, the magic began, and Reisman hired him.

A year after Dad started in the big time, Leo Reisman left the Waldorf for the Central Park Casino, and brought Eddy along.

Dad had, or made, his big break at the Casino, which was said to have been the greatest nightclub of them all. The building was torn down before I was born, yet from what I've read, I'm inclined to agree. The Casino was a fabulous club with a short lifespan: it opened in 1929 during Prohibition; and closed in 1934, the year after liquor became legal again. The place was the essence of glamour. The décor was stunning; the guests, their clothes and jewelry were the top of the top; and the near nightly patronage of Mayor Jimmy Walker created a frisson of excitement.

The club was located just off the east side of the 72nd Street transverse, a beautiful spot in every season. No other place in New York could create such a setting. The original building was designed by one of the park's landscape architects, Calvert Vaux, and opened in 1864. Named the Ladies' Refreshment Salon, its purpose was to serve unaccompanied women, which meant that they were not accompanied by a man. More recently, the site had been leased to what *The New Yorker* described as "a somewhat dumpy nite-club."

Central Park was owned by the city and Jimmy Walker, often dubbed "the night mayor" because of his propensity for long nights out and short days at the office, made certain the lease would not be renewed. His friend Sidney Solomon was granted a new lease to establish a club where those he described as "the fashionable and the fastidious" could dine and dance. Solomon was rumored to have ingratiated himself to the mayor by introducing him to his tailor. That might be true; Jimmy was so obsessed with his wardrobe that on one occasion his valet packed forty-three suits for a trip to Europe.

Solomon initially planned to establish a private club. The mayor would be an unofficial member, making it less vulnerable to raids by Prohibition officers. Furthermore, liquor wouldn't be sold, or technically, served. Guests would bring their own Champagne or booze, and leave the bottles in their cars. When they were ready for a refill, the maître d' would signal to their chauffeurs, who would appear with the bottles to be handed over to the chauffeur's boss.

The club was to be overseen by a board of governors, men of social and show business standing, who would provide the necessary cachet, and attract a desirable clientele. The chairman of the board was the old-name socialite Anthony J. Drexel Biddle Jr.; William Rhinelander Stewart also added social prestige: the Rhinelanders were an old colonial family. (When telephone exchanges had names, the Casino's number was Rhinelander 4-3040.) Another member of the board, Florenz Ziegfeld of the *Ziegfeld Follies,* promised to send "Follies girls" over after the legal 3:00 a.m. closing time. To be sure they wouldn't be stopped, Walker would arrange a police escort.

The idea was ripe, but even the mayor couldn't change the law that made it illegal to site a private entity on public land. Instead, the Casino was recast as a nightclub; the same governors remained in place, and the air of exclusivity was only partly diminished.

Joseph Urban, the Viennese designer who planned sets for the Metropolitan Opera and the Ziegfeld Theatre, was hired to create the most magnificent club in the United States, preferably the entire world. His masterpiece was the Art Deco ballroom where Dad would later play. The ceiling, paneled in large squares of black mirror, was hung with enormous crystal chandeliers, which with their unshaded electrified candles created "a circular constellation in the black glass above." Men in black or white tie and women wearing couture evening gowns were faintly reflected in the mirrors as they danced. The glass ceiling was an acoustical triumph. As *The Architectural Record* reported in a twelve-page illustrated feature in the August 1929 issue, "The music has a sharp brilliance. . . . Such power is given to the tone that it penetrates the whole building when not muffled by the presence of many people."

I wonder how Dad felt when he first saw, and played, in that ballroom. When I was a child, he was a celebrity, but in 1929 he was only twenty, six years younger than I was when I started at the Maisonette. Night after night, he would be exposed to a roomful of strangers, social and show business icons, and the mayor of the city. Maybe even then, he was so naturally confident that he believed he belonged there. As it turned out, he did.

The Casino was such a big deal that its opening made front-page news all over the country, although there was no mention of Eddy Duchin. He was still just an anonymous member of the band.

Newspapers reported that 2,400 people had received invitations, but so many people had accepted that the board of governors was faced with a dilemma: how to cut the list to a bulging six hundred without making the others so angry they wouldn't patronize the place, even when they could. The board didn't have to worry.

The Casino continued to make news, and after a while Eddy began to gain traction. It happened like this: during breaks, when the other musicians in the Reisman band went out for a smoke, Dad, who never smoked, stayed on and continued to play. Maybe he wasn't sure what else to do during the breaks, and it's pretty certain that he hoped to be noticed, which he was. He wasn't just playing background cocktail piano, and he had the kind of personality and strikingly good looks that naturally attract attention. Guests began to come over to the piano to hear him, watch him play, share a joke or a compliment, and tell their friends about the glamorous young man with "the magic fingers."

Within three years, Dad had replaced Reisman. Andy Wiswell, who played trombone in Dad's orchestra, described his effect on the Casino's patronage. Seven nights a week, he said, "the rope was up. . . . And that was all the more remarkable when you realize that people had to be dressed formally to be allowed into the place." The invitation to the 1932 opening of the Casino featured a photograph of my father above bold type featuring EDDIE [*sic*] DUCHIN AND HIS ORCHESTRA. That was quite a coup: the composer Jerome Kern once called the Reisman Orchestra "The String Quartet of Dance Bands."

Dad was twenty-two.

The Night Mayor

JIMMY WALKER GAVE THE casino a lot of its prestige. Night after night, when he arrived with his mistress, the showgirl Betty Compton, the headwaiter signaled to my father, and the band smoothly moved into Walker's theme song, "Will you love me in December / as you do in May," which the mayor wrote back in 1909. Fortunately, that's the only one of his tunes that has survived.

Unlike most of his constituents during the Depression, Walker was making stacks of money. He did his personal business in an office on the Casino's second floor. Other rooms for friends and their "dates" were down the hall. The mayor called the Casino his "uptown office," and City Hall his "downtown office." His room was a kind of bank, with deposits made directly to him. His connections extended deep into the underworld: the prominent gangster Arnold Rothstein, who fixed the 1919 World Series, reputedly invested $500,000 in the renovation of the club. Bootlegging was big business in the underworld; maybe Rothstein expected to get part of his investment back by selling cases of the best quality booze to the club's patrons.

Rothstein was purportedly F. Scott Fitzgerald's model for Meyer Wolfsheim in *The Great Gatsby*. Gatsby's house in the fictional West Egg on Long Island has been said to have been based on the Pulitzer Prize–winning journalist and *New York World* editor Herbert Bayard Swope's "Lands End, Prospect Point," which was within walking distance of the Harrimans' summer place in Sands Point. Fitzgerald, who rented a house across the bay, was often among the Swopes' guests, but whether Gatsby's house was invented by Fitzgerald or based on an existing house has been a matter of some conjecture; in any case, experts on Fitzgerald's works have determined that it wasn't modeled on Lands End.

An old newspaper clipping indicates how Jimmy Walker worked, although his name isn't mentioned. It appears that he had tipped off a business partner that the city planned to fill in an underwater area in Jamaica, Queens, to make a park. His partner bought the "useless" site for $60,000, waited four years until the park project was in an early stage, and offered to sell it to the city for $1 million. The experts valued it at $170,000. The New York State Supreme Court called the partner to testify and asked for six years of his tax returns. He refused and was cited for contempt of court. I'd guess the contempt ruling disappeared.

Maybe Dad knew what was going on upstairs, and maybe he didn't. I doubt that he was part of the deals, and not just because he was my father. His business was music, he was on a fast, upward trajectory, he was making plenty of money, and he didn't want or need to get involved with gangsters.

The mayor's private transactions became so public that Governor Franklin D. Roosevelt could have required that he be investigated for corruption by the Seabury Commission, named after Samuel Seabury, the then-former judge of the court of appeals, but Roosevelt had a problem. Although as mayor, Walker had substantially improved the city's infrastructure and social services, he was indisputably corrupt. Yet, he had made the nominating speech for FDR in 1928, and the governor was running for office again in '32. If the flamboyant mayor was in the news, his connection with the governor could be damaging. Daily reports about Jimmy's assuredly colorful testimony would almost certainly overshadow newspaper coverage of the campaign. Instead, FDR permitted Walker to resign, and in 1931 "the night mayor" and his mistress (and later wife), Betty Compton, sailed to France.

THE DAY THE MUSIC STOPPED

THE MUSIC AT THE Casino went silent a couple of years after the populist Fiorello La Guardia was appointed to replace Jimmy Walker. Splurging at a luxurious nightclub was out of joint with conditions in the rest of America. The stock market crash may have thinned out the Casino's guests, but it cleaned out people all over the country.

Communism had begun to sound appealing among certain literati, artists, and even socialites. John D. Rockefeller Jr. commissioned the Mexican artist Diego Rivera to paint a massive mural for the lobby of 30 Rockefeller

Center, but when Rivera portrayed communist leaders, including Lenin, Rockefeller was outraged. He demanded that his son Nelson get rid of the work immediately, and by any possible means. The building was closed for the night, the work was dismantled, and the pieces were dumped in the East River. I've heard that the deed was done by the next morning.

In 1932, while Dad was still playing "Night and Day" and "April in Paris" for habitués of the Casino, Bing Crosby introduced the song "Brother, Can You Spare A Dime?," and Irving Berlin wrote the Depression-era "Let's Have Another Cup of Coffee."

La Guardia found the contrast between bread lines and a famously expensive nightclub odious. Robert Moses, the master city planner and power broker, who, it was rumored, was once turned away from the Casino, pressured the mayor to close the club. It was torn down in 1935, the year my parents were married. The site was reconfigured as the two-acre Mary Harriman Rumsey Playfield for children, named after Averell's sister, who died in a riding accident in 1934.

If the building that housed the Casino were still standing, it would be no more than an artifact from the past, rented for weddings, other big events, or a 1930s-themed costume parties. The Casino was a one-off; there's never been its like again.

"Buck, Buck, Bucket . . ."

THE CASINO WAS CLOSED, but Dad was on a roll. He made one successful record after another; introduced ten-inch album sets with four or more discs; and presented such then-unknown singers as Mary Martin.

Studio recordings, with take after take, are often tedious. That's how the Eddy Duchin Orchestra "scandal" got started. The band had repeated the tune "Ol' Man Mose" by Louis Armstrong so many times that the mischievous singer Patricia Norman replaced the refrain "buck, buck, bucket" with "fuck, fuck, fuck-it." The record was released; radio stations picked up the "mistake," and it was recalled and rerecorded. Nevertheless, it became Dad's biggest hit.

Radio spread Dad's name and music far beyond big city ballrooms. In 1930, radios were centerpieces in 12 million homes; and their programs were available to 40 percent of Americans; ten years later, the number had soared to 83 percent. During the Depression, when one third of the country's movie theaters closed because so few people could afford the twenty-five-cent tickets—a dollar for a family of four—radio provided free entertainment. One writer described the radio as "the electronic hearth." The least expensive sets cost under $40 (about $780 in current dollars), but could be paid off in installments.

If only one family in a neighborhood could afford to buy a set, friends would come over to listen. A few powerful stations had the wattage to transmit nationwide; one, located just over the border in Mexico to avoid U.S. regulations, transmitted at 500,000 watts. It was said that the cowboys in Texas could pick up the shows from the barbed wire fencing. When newly elected president Franklin D. Roosevelt made his famous March 12, 1933, radio speech, announcing short-term bank closings to prevent further failures, 60 million Americans listened.

Big Band music, often broadcast live from ballrooms, flooded the airways and featured Dad and other great bandleaders, among them Tommy Dorsey, Glenn Miller, Duke Ellington, and Benny Goodman. Like Dad, they were part of shows that included singers and comedians like Jack Benny, or Peter Lind Hayes and Mary Healey. Dad and Bing Crosby also hosted the successful *Kraft Music Hall,* which featured both well-known and upcoming guests. Nat King Cole, an excellent pianist, played and sang on the show with his trio, and during one of the breaks, Dad advised him to concentrate on his distinctive voice. Others probably made the same suggestion. We know how that turned out.

Some bands had commercial sponsors, who used them—and vice versa—to publicize their products. A banner above the bandstand at Glenn Miller's performances read "Glenn Miller and His Chesterfield Orchestra," and included an image of a cigarette. Record companies backed top bands, which spread their fame even more widely.

In 1940, eight years after the Casino closed, when Dad was contracted for the first of a series of six-month gigs at the Waldorf's fabulous Starlight Roof, he was paid $5,000 a week, which exceeded the fees earned by some of the greatest actors of his time. The same year, Jimmy Stewart took home $3,000 a week for his role in *The Philadelphia Story,* for which he was awarded an Oscar as Best Actor.

I've often worked in the same places as my father: among them, the Palmer House in Chicago, where he was performing when I was born, the Waldorf, and the Cocoanut Grove in the Ambassador Hotel in Los Angeles. One night when I was at the Cocoanut Grove, Cary Grant and his wife came to hear me. When they got up to dance, I played "We are poor little lambs," the song Cole Porter wrote for the Yale singing group the Whiffenpoofs, when Cole was a student there. Cary had been in *Monkey Business* with Ginger Rogers, and they had danced a romantic dance to that tune. When he came over to say hello, I told him I'd let him off easy because I didn't play the really fast Dixieland number he danced in *Indiscreet*.

It always gives me pleasure to know that, decades apart, my father and I were, in a sense, leading our bands together. Maybe some of the pianos were unchanged, and we had run our fingers over the same keys.

Both of us also played at the White House. President Franklin D. Roosevelt chose the Eddy Duchin Orchestra for his inaugural ball. Lyndon Johnson picked my band for one of his inaugural balls, and for both Luci's and Lynda Johnson's weddings. When Jimmy Carter was elected, I organized the music for his six balls, and I played at George H. W. Bush's inauguration, as well as at many other White House parties.

I also play many of the same tunes my father did, but our styles are quite different. In 1935, Dad told George T. Simon in *The Big Bands,* "I close my eyes, hum to myself and then play what I happen to feel inside me." His sound was more melodic, while mine has undertones of jazz. Dad also pretty much stuck to written arrangements, as I did when I started, but I soon began to improvise. Now, I rarely use charts.

Among the characteristics we have in common is how

attuned we are to the dancers. Dad told Simon, "You must remember all the time . . . that your dance music is for dancing primarily. If the crowd finds your music easy to dance to, then you're a success." That's as true today as it was in the 1930s.

At the end of 1999, I saw in the new millennium at a New Year's Eve party at the Ritz hotel in Boston, another place where Dad had played. We'd "crossed paths" many times, but the moment when the 1900s changed to the 2000s marked a clear, if not final, dividing line between his era and mine.

THE LADIES IN HIS LIFE

WHEN DAD RETURNED FROM Brazil after my mother's death, he was booked for months at a time for jobs all over the country. The Cocoanut Grove was one of his regular gigs, and he was soon incorporated into the movie community, which included some pretty snappy women. The reason I know about at least some of them is that, over the years, they have more or less told me.

My band likes to remind me about the times when a woman of my father's generation approaches the bandstand, looks me deep in the eyes, and announces, "I knew your father." I say "How great!" To be sure I understand, she'll add, "I mean, I *really knew* your father." What am I supposed to do? Ask her "How was he?" The real eye-opener took place when we were hired to play at the Beverly Hills Hotel at a party to honor the movie star Lana Turner. Lana, who was married eight times to seven different husbands (she married one of them twice), used to say that her goal was to have one husband and seven children, but it had turned out the opposite way. A lot of former stars were at the party, and although I've absolutely forbidden members of the band to photograph guests, they couldn't resist. It was hard to believe some of the stars were still alive. Many of them looked pretty good.

On my way to the bandstand that night, an attractive woman with dark hair and eyelashes as long as a camel's came over and introduced herself as Dorothy Lamour, the singer and actress who was famous for appearing in the series of movies known as "The Road to . . ." (as in, *The Road to Bali*). She gave me a Hollywood smile, opened her eyes wide, and announced, "I knew your father well." To make herself absolutely clear, she said, "We spent a lot of time together." Then, I really did want to know "how he was."

HOLLYWOOD 1946

THE WAR WAS OVER, it was 1946, and Dad and three friends decided to give a party—not just any party, but "the party of the century." The friends were Cary Grant, Jimmy Stewart, and the columnist John McClain.

They sent the invitation by telegram, just one week in advance. It read:

WE FIGURE IT'S ABOUT TIME WE THREW
A PARTY, SO WILL YOU COME TO THE
OLD CLOVER CLUB, 8477 SUNSET BOULEVARD,
8 PM, NEXT SATURDAY, MARCH 30TH.
SORRY ABOUT THE SHORT NOICE BUT WE'VE

ONLY JUST BEEN ABLE TO HIRE THE JOINT.
PLEASE ANSWER EARLY.
WE ARE NERVOUS. BLACK TIE, LOW CUT
DRESSES. ARDMORE 8-6056. EDDY DUCHIN,
CARY GRANT, JOHN MCCLAIN
AND JIMMY STEWART.

The Clover Club, located in a sleek white Art Deco building, was a nightclub with a louche reputation: it was also an illegal gambling establishment, regularly raided by vice squad deputies, who sometimes wore tuxedoes to blend in. It had, in fact been raided as recently as the October before the party—which didn't seem to make any difference to its popularity.

Some of the guests stayed nearby at the Garden of Allah, a small hotel with twenty-five villas. The main building was the home of the silent screen star Alla Nazimova who bought the elaborate mansion on Sunset Boulevard in 1919. Among its eccentricities was her swimming pool, made in the shape of the Black Sea, which was near her childhood home in Russia. When her career waned, she built the villas, and turned her home into a hotel.

In 1927, Alla decided the hospitality business was not for her. She sold the place, and it became even more exclusive and very private. Laurence Olivier, Gary Cooper, Leopold Stravinsky, and F. Scott Fitzgerald were among the many celebrities who stayed there. Each night, guests meandered from villa to villa, to and from parties, which were not known for their decorum. The writer and comedian Robert Benchley was a sometime resident, and had arranged that if he was drunk, he would be loaded into a wheelbarrow, and moved along to the next villa. "Take me to the Black Sea," he would call out. One of my favorite Benchley stories, of which there are many, is of the cable he sent to Dorothy Parker from Venice. If I remember right, he wrote "The streets are filled with water. Please advise."

The hosts and the Hollywood location of the party were irresistible. Whitneys and Vanderbilts, and of course, Marie and Ave flew out or took the train across the country to California. Movie stars included Humphrey Bogart, Spencer Tracy, Charlie Chaplin, Douglas Fairbanks Jr., Bob Hope, Bing Crosby, and on and on.

It was a dream list for the readers of movie magazines, and made terrific copy for Hedda Hopper, the gossip columnist who wrote the syndicated column "Hedda Hopper's Hollywood," read by 35 million Americans. I've been to and played at enough parties to know that there's no such thing as "the party of the century," but if that wasn't at least the party of its decade, I don't know what was.

GOOD TIMES

ALL THIS WAS HAPPENING beyond my purview. I was old enough to know that Dad was a celebrity, but what I really cared about was that he was my father, and he wasn't living up to the job. In fairness, I believe he made a pretty big effort, but for some reason he didn't seem to know how to get along with a kid. We did share a passion for baseball and he took me to games when he could. Our running argument was about who was better: the Yanks' Joe DiMaggio or the Red Sox's Ted Williams; but we never tossed a ball around in the backyard, the way I later did with my kids. Maybe Dad wanted to protect his hands.

Dad knew some of the players, which is how I came to meet Joe DiMaggio. One summer day, I came home to find the great center-fielder sitting in our garden. I can't remember what either of us said—certainly not much, as I was starstruck. I think he gave me a baseball glove. I wish I still had it.

Many years after Joe retired, I ran across him in an airport when he was changing planes. He waved at me and said, "Hi, Peter." The band never let me forget it. One of the guys said, "I suppose you know Monroe, too, boss," but I didn't answer.

Our best times were on our rare vacations together. One Christmas, Dad and Chiq took me to Sun Valley. I'd been skiing there all my short life, and I got a kick out of watching Dad, who was a beginner. He wasn't much of an athlete, but he sure gave it a shot. Chiq had skied before and she did just fine. Although my father wasn't a success on the slopes, he was in his element at night. I've always remembered the time they took me to a party at the Trail Creek Cabin, a charmingly cozy spot that had been built for entertaining. We rode to the cabin in a horse-drawn sleigh, snuggled under piles of fur blankets, holding on to each other. That was probably the closest together the three of us had ever been. When we arrived at Trail Creek, the place was full of Dad and Chiq's friends. After dinner, Dad went over to the piano and started to play. I was proud to see the guests gathering around to listen to him, and I crowded in with the others. Dad was elated; he loved playing the piano and he loved entertaining people. Tyrone Power was at the party and, later, I thought of that night when I saw Ty playing Dad in *The Eddy Duchin Story*. I've often gone back to Sun Valley, and when I've taken the sleigh to the cabin, I think of that sweet night.

THE LAST TUNE

WE HAD TWO PIANOS in the house in Manhasset. I'm sure Dad and I would have become closer through music, and that he hoped we would play duets one day. We gave it a try a couple of times when I was young, but I was a rough beginner. I listened to him when he practiced, and I couldn't imagine I would ever be nearly as good, or even be in the same profession, but I looked forward to the day when I could play well enough for us to perform those duets, if only for fun.

On a February day in 1951, the Eaglebrook headmaster called me into his study. He told me I would be taking the train to New York that afternoon, and that the school chaplain would accompany me. He didn't explain why I was leaving and I was afraid I was in trouble.

I disembarked at Grand Central Station, where the Harrimans' driver usually met me. This time, Averell was waiting on the platform. He was wearing a long dark coat and hat, and looked very severe. Ave was a superb diplomat, but even for him, it must have been a challenge to tell a motherless twelve-year-old boy that his father had died. Dad was only forty-one.

After Dad's death, Chiquita sold the house and most of the furnishings, but she saved one of the baby grands for me. That's the Bechstein that lives on in Virginia and my living room.

A "REAL" FATHER

DESPITE HIS EFFORTS TO be a real father, I had to face the evidence that Dad was more interested in himself and his career than in me. Many fathers of his generation had a rather formal relationship with their children, but at least they were usually home for dinner, awake for breakfast, went to their kids' games and school plays and parents' days, and met with their teachers to discuss their grades and progress. Dad wasn't always working, and he could have done some of those things, but he didn't.

I was well into my forties when my band was playing near where my childhood nurse Chissy lived; we hadn't been in touch for decades, but I called and told her I'd like to see her. She said she'd be happy if I came over. I was so young when she left that I only had a vague feeling of warmth and a sense of curiosity when I thought about her, but we got along right away, she shared her memories with me and we had a good visit.

After I returned home, I received a letter from her, which I've saved. Chissy bluntly confirmed what I suppose I knew, but never wanted to admit to myself. She described Dad as "very self-absorbed, unpredictable, quick-tempered, inappreciative, always concerned about expenses," "but," she added, "he could be thoughtful and charming when he wanted to be." She understood how depressed he had been after my mother died, but, she wrote, "What did surprise and annoy me was that his lack of attention to you lasted so long." Although I stayed in the hospital for many months after I was born, the first time Chissy remembered Dad visiting me was when I was eight or nine months old, something that, in hindsight, I find absolutely unbelievable.

As for my parents, I always assumed that they had a storybook romance. I began to consider how their relationship might have developed had she lived. When I was away from home, at Hotchkiss, my mother would have been about forty. Maybe she would have become tired of waiting around for Dad during the long, late nights when he was performing, and the weeks when he was booked in another city. She had always been independent; she had friends in many parts of society, had traveled extensively, and she could have gotten along on her own. I wouldn't be surprised if she had fallen out of love with the narcissist I now recognize my father to have been, and wanted a chance to start again.

She wasn't given that choice. I don't have a choice either. Even now, when I look at my father's pictures, I miss him. But I missed him when he was alive.

Intermezzo

My Cane

I WAS READY TO resume a reasonably normal life after nearly a year of rehab, and as soon as I felt safe and steady enough to walk using a cane, I began to go out to favorite restaurants and my club, a relief after months of hospital food; visited art galleries, often with Virginia; and attended rehearsals at the Metropolitan Opera. Each excursion, each friend seen again seemed exciting and fresh.

The first time I took the crosstown bus, I was exhilarated, until a young woman saw my cane, stood up, and offered me her seat. That was something new! Maybe I had become an old codger. I'd lost a lot of weight, and I moved more deliberately than I had before. My hair had become grayer, and I felt different, but evidently I didn't look as different as I thought. Occasionally a stranger would say "Hi," as we passed on the street. One man even stopped me to ask if it was too late for him to start taking piano lessons. I began to give him the conventional "You're never too old" answer, but he really wanted to know, so I added, "You can do it, and if you get anywhere, you'll have a hell of a lot of fun."

Old Friends, New Stories

MOST DAYS, I HAD lunch with friends. I enjoyed picking up where we'd left off, but our conversations often took unexpected directions. My disabilities seem to have broken down their reserve, and people I'd known for decades opened up. A playwright with whom I've traveled and had years of enjoyable meals, discussing the theater, books, politics, and people, had a heart attack around the time of my stroke. He looked fine, but when I asked what he was working on, he admitted that he hadn't written anything for a year: "Too depressed." Recently, he had agreed to write a magazine article, and hoped it would get him going again, but he was dreading the prospect of producing even a short piece. I guess he felt I would understand what it's like when you can't do the very thing that has always gotten you up in the morning, and kept you up late at night.

Sometimes my lunch companions were women I'd kept in touch with since I played at their deb parties and weddings. Those conversations, too, could turn interesting corners, as they told me stories I had never heard or imagined. An attractive woman who had had a fabulous party confessed that she sometimes felt awkward—"gawky" was the word she used—on the dance floor. She stands around 5'11" and at her coming-out party, when all the boys were expected to ask her to dance, she dreaded seeing a guy coming toward her who just reached her shoulders. "It started in dancing school," she said. "You want to hear my mother's advice? She told me 'Just think of this: you could eat crackers off his head.'"

I laughed. "Did it help?"

"Are you kidding?" she said.

A legendary book editor who had grown up in the South told me about the pressure placed on girls to "let the boys do the talking." She remembered leaving a dinner before a dance, when the hostess's mother whispered, "Now, young ladies, remember: put your brains in your pockets." That attitude wasn't a regional peculiarity. An extremely nearsighted woman from New York, who had always been popular, confessed that her mother insisted that she leave her glasses home when she went to a party. It wasn't only that the glasses spoiled her "look"; they made her seem too smart.

Boys who weren't all that confident themselves could make the girls feel uncomfortable. At Yale, I knew two brothers who were only eighteen months apart, and closely resembled each other. We were often at the same parties, but I'd never noticed anything unusual about their behavior. A woman who had been the butt of one of their jokes told me that sometimes if they were at dances held at houses nearby, they seized the opportunity to change places during the midnight supper, and drove at top speed over to the other's party. She hadn't known them well, and when she was confronted with the "wrong" brother, she was confused. She'd always been embarrassed to confess that they'd fooled her. In retrospect, she was angry: young men playing tricks on girls might have seemed amusing then, at least to them. Not anymore.

Many of the women who told me those stories are grandmothers. Why did they suddenly confide in me? Maybe when they recalled the parties where I'd played, they had remembered an unapproachably "glamorous older man" (in my twenties!), just out of reach on the bandstand. Now I was disabled, and none of us had anything to hide.

GETTING AROUND

MY OUTINGS BECAME MORE ambitious. I revisited my favorite museums, and discovered others I'd never heard of. Like many kids, I'd had fantasies of being a spy, and one afternoon, a couple of friends and I visited the KGB Espionage Museum on West 14th Street, where a private collection of some 3,500 objects was on display. I'd seen James Bond movies and read some spy books, but I was amazed by the array of instruments I would have been up against if I'd entered the secret world. I was particularly amused by part of a dinner service, which had tiny microphones hidden in the base of the plates.

My principal contact with Russians was in quite a different context. One year, I played for the White Russian New Year's Eve ball, where many of the guests are descendants of former nobility. The evening became very lively after my friend Serge Obolensky performed a traditional sword dance. In the days of the czars, the Russians could be pretty tricky, but whatever eavesdropping they did was more subtle and personal. Unfortunately, the KGB museum is now closed; its contents, including the plates, were auctioned in February 2021.

One of my early post-stroke expeditions was to visit some of my favorite works of art by Sol LeWitt and Richard Serra at the Dia Foundation, upstate along the Hudson River in Beacon, New York. The July before I had my stroke, the foundation had hired me to play at the artist Walter De Maria's memorial service there. Walter's favorite tune was "Peace, Peace," a beautiful jazz improvisation composed by my favorite jazz pianist, Bill Evans.

Dia had commissioned Walter's most famous installation, *The Lightning Field,* a work of Land Art installed in undeveloped grasslands on a plateau in New Mexico's remote high desert. Four hundred polished stainless steel poles, each around twenty feet high and two inches in diameter, are spaced two feet apart in a massive horizontal grid measuring one mile by one kilometer. In his *New Yorker* piece "Poles Apart: Notes from a Pilgrimage," the journalist and author Geoff Dyer put it this way: "Planted in the Earth and reaching toward the sky, they call down its power—literally creating man-made lightning storms." I've always wanted to see *The Lightning Field* and I hoped I'd soon be ready to go.

Walter was a musician as well as an artist. At the age of eleven, he joined a local musicians' union in California as a pianist and percussionist. In New York, he became the drummer in an alternative rock group, The Primitives, whose members included Lou Reed and John Cale. The Primitives melded into The Velvet Underground, the house band at The Factory, Andy Warhol's headquarters.

While I was confined to the hospital and at home, I missed hearing live music. As soon as I was mobile, I began to attend the Metropolitan Opera's morning dress rehearsals, a tradition with many opera buffs. I like seeing an opera before opening night: the singers don't sing at full volume, but you can watch them growing into their parts. I'm amused at how many people bring box lunches to eat in the restaurant on the Grand Tier during intermissions. The restaurant is closed at that time of day, but the chairs and tables are set out. As soon as members of the audience arrive, show their tickets, and pass through the turnstile, they race to the Grand Tier to nab a seat, where they leave their food and sometimes their coats. I usually wait until the opera is over, and have lunch in a restaurant across the street.

I was getting around on my own now, but my left hand was still barely functional. I didn't know if I'd ever be able to enjoy my other passion: I wanted to get out on the river again.

CAMP HARMONY

I GREW UP FISHING for large-mouth bass in one of the lakes on the Harrimans' property at Arden, but what I like best is to wade in a stream, and cast a fly to a rising trout. I'm entirely focused, looking for the feeding fish; watching the rippling of the water skirting around rocks and flowing on; the hatch of bugs skittering along the surface; the subtle hum of nature; and the fading light, as the long summer days fold up.

The smell, the sound, and the beauty of the surroundings transport me the way music does. Often, when I'm fishing, I hear music in my mind; sometimes Mozart sonatas; or jazz tunes like "I Remember Clifford," written about the great trumpet player Clifford Brown, and played by Lee Morgan.

The summer after my stroke, I wasn't sure I had the strength or the balance to accept a friend's invitation to fish at Camp Harmony, a private club established in 1895 on the Restigouche River in Canada. I was inspired by the thought of a woman I knew quite well, who still fished when she was over ninety. She waded into the Big Wood

River in Sun Valley, while her guide kept his arm around her so she wouldn't slip and fall. Then she cast a fly; if she rose a trout, she retrieved it, and sometimes they landed it.

If that old girl could pull a trout out of a river, I was damned if I couldn't do it, too. I've fished with my three kids since they were very young and they all like to fish, and do it well. Over the years, we've probably had as many laughs as fish. My younger son, Colin, was an ideal companion, and I asked him to join me on the Restigouche. The handsome log lodge was rather surprisingly designed by the architect Stanford White, best known for marble mansions like Rosecliff, which he built for my ancestors the Oelrichses in Newport. The porch overlooks the river, and at the end of the day, guests sit in rocking chairs with drinks and swap stories. Lies abound, and so does whiskey. About ten of us were there that week, and we all ate at the same table in the big room, with a huge roaring fire in a fireplace built of large stones from the river.

The long, motorized canoes we use have a seat with a back; and Colin and I worked out a good partnership. On a drop, I cast as far as I could from a sitting position, then handed the rod to Colin, who easily cast thirty-odd feet further. If we raised a salmon, he played it, then released it, because my left hand wasn't strong enough to hold the rod with a powerful fighting fish on the end. I'd been afraid I would never be able to fish again; instead, I found a way to do what I love, and do it with my son.

I had had a serious stroke, and I'd gone on a fishing expedition within a year. I was reminded of my friend the late businessman and amateur cellist Jimmy Wolfensohn, who asked me to join the board of Carnegie Hall when he was chairman. Jimmy had had a stroke before I did, and he often came to see me in the hospital. He encouraged me not to let the stroke get me down, but to get out and take risks.

That's what I'd just done, and I was feeling pretty proud of myself.

BACK INTO THE VOID, NOVEMBER 2014

VIRGINIA AND I RESUMED our usual pattern: weekdays in town, and most weekends at Virginia's charming small house in a village on the eastern end of Long Island. In late November 2014, when I was in the country, I tried to climb the two steps from our terrace to the house, and stumbled. My balance was slow to return and I felt a little wobbly. I was still off balance on Sunday when we drove back to the city.

Early Monday morning, I fell again, this time in my room. I crawled back to my bed, called out to Virginia for help, blacked out, had a seizure, and went into convulsions.

Once more, I was in an ambulance, and then in the ICU, where the doctors induced a coma to prevent brain damage. When I was moved into a private room, Virginia, the kids, and Adelle visited me. They didn't know if a person in a coma could hear what was going on, but the doctors told them to talk to me. Jason later reported that he'd told me he'd taken all my fishing equipment, and thanked me for the gift. If anything could have jolted me awake, that would have done it, but I remained artificially comatose for a few more days.

The doctors gradually brought me back to a conscious

state. I awakened to find my family standing around, anticipating my return. When I said, "What's going on? Where the hell am I? And what are you all doing here?" it seemed that I was going to be okay.

Sometimes everything happens at once: Virginia was in the hospital on the way to see me when she fell on a slippery floor and fractured her ankle. There went another Thanksgiving.

THE BOXES

THE SEIZURE WAS ANOTHER warning that anything could happen to me at any time, and I started to think seriously about how much longer I'd be around. The pictures of my parents had awakened my curiosity and I thought of a jumble of cardboard boxes that I'd held on to for decades, and which might be worth exploring. I hadn't looked through them in ages, but I knew more or less what was in them: memorabilia from the Central Park Casino, nightclubs, private parties, and charity balls. They were artifacts of a singular era of live music and dancing, glamour and Society.

The contents of those taped-up boxes ignited another kind of post-illness awakening, this time about the life I've led and the world in which I've lived. I could have thrown the boxes out—after all, I hadn't been particularly interested in excavating them before. Instead, I opened them to see where they led.

PART THREE

REFLECTIONS
IN A
REARVIEW MIRROR

"O tempora! O mores"
(Oh, the times! Oh, the customs!)

The first time I appeared in public, I was a twenty-two-year-old private, one of the winners of an Army talent contest. We appeared on *The Ed Sullivan Show,* watched by more than 60 million viewers, who accounted for 82.6 percent of the television audience.

It was the biggest audience I would ever have.

CHAPTER NINE

Becoming
Peter Duchin

"T.V.: EDDY DUCHIN'S SON"

I JOINED THE ARMY as a private in 1959, and was sent to Fort Jackson, South Carolina. Believe me, Basic Training had nothing to do with playing the piano, or music. Then, one night, I'd had a few drinks and was playing on an old upright in an off-base bar. My commanding officer heard me, and asked if he could enter me in the Army talent contest. I said sure, and I won.

That late August, I was sent to New York with winners from Army units all over the country. We would be featured on the hugely popular *Ed Sullivan Show,* which aired on CBS at 8:00 on Sunday nights and regularly attracted 60 million viewers. That would be the biggest audience I'd have in a very long career.

It was no small thing to be "the talent." In 1956, Ed had featured the controversially sexy new pop star Elvis Presley receiving a polio shot on air, to demonstrate that the vaccine was safe. The thirteen-year-old classical violin genius Itzhak Perlman made his television debut on the show in 1958. The Army winners followed the next year. That was a bit of a come-down, but a sentimental fondness for "our boys in uniform" gave us a boost.

Steve Lawrence, the official vocal soloist with the United States Army Band, sang "Day In, Day Out" and "If I Loved You." He would become a successful singer and actor with his wife, Eydie Gormé. I was on next, shaking nervously in the wings, when Sullivan called me onto the stage and introduced me as "Eddy Duchin's son!"

I played what I thought was expected of me: Dad's theme, "To Love Again," based on Chopin's Nocturne in E-flat; and the seasonally appropriate "Summertime." Ed's terrific bandleader Ray Bloch kindly kept time with me, which I'm sure made me sound better than I was. (Ray had a well-known sense of humor. Once when Duke Ellington was on the show, Duke put the music in front of him, and said "A-Train." Ray turned to the band and told them they were going to play "a train.")

In retrospect, "The Jamaicans," the act that followed me, was a much bigger deal: Army regiments had only become integrated after World War II, and five Black soldiers who had formed the vocal group sang "Jamaica Farewell."

The next morning, *New York Times* television critic John P. Shanley's two-column review was headlined "T.V.: Eddy Duchin's Son," with the subhead "Soldier-Pianist Plays Father's Theme in Sullivan Show Appearance." The story opened "Most of the excitement on last night's 'Ed Sullivan Show' over Channel 2 was caused by the appearance of a young soldier-pianist named Peter Duchin." Shanley went on to critique my performance, writing that while it was "brief, but enjoyable. . . . His style at the keyboard is not yet so authoritative as his father's was. But," he added, "he has time on his side. He is 22 years old and handsome enough to attract attention without the benefit of music." I was a little disappointed that he was more enthusiastic about my looks than my ability at the piano.

A PIANIST IN UNIFORM

I COMPLETED BASIC TRAINING and was sent to Panama, which I thought was a mysterious military mismatch. I had scored 100 percent on my Army French exam, and had hoped to serve in Paris at SHAPE (Supreme Headquarters Allied Powers Europe). Instead: Panama? I quickly learned that the country and my assignment there were more interesting than I had expected.

I was billeted in Fort Clayton, an Army camp in the Canal Zone, about eight miles from Panama City. The barracks were three-story screened buildings with concrete floors, lined with bunks with green foot lockers at one end. I did everything the other privates did, and was also assigned to play the glockenspiel in the Army band. The bandleader was a three-hundred-pound warrant officer named Adam Schpekowsky with a limited musical repertoire: he played the clarinet in a polka band in civilian life. Adam was leery of me at first. He had seen my papers, which, he later told me, had POLITICAL INFLU-ENCE stamped all over them. Obviously, Ave had put in a word for me when I was hoping to be sent to Paris. Wherever those decisions are made, the "influence" was either ignored or irritated someone. Instead of reliving my time in France, I was marching in hundred-degree weather, carrying a heavy instrument stuck into a belt around my waist, and striking the metal keys with a wooden mallet, producing a penetrating sound.

In addition to the official Army band, a group of us, along with musicians from the nearby Air Force base, created our own jazz and Latin band. We were encouraged to play around town, in parks, squares, and hospitals, including a facility for people with mental illness. We began to notice that one man turned up quite regularly at our impromptu concerts, and we got to know him a bit. His name was George Hyatt, but he was called "Slim," for obvious reasons. After a while, he started to help us set up, and we discovered that he knew a lot of jazz, Latin, and popular music. Slim became a friend, and when I returned to New York, I helped him get immigration papers. A few years later, he would become an unexpectedly important figure in the music world.

The Zone, which separated two parts of Panama, had been an unincorporated territory of the United States since 1904. The Panamanians wanted the Americans to turn the Zone over to them and go home. At the least, they insisted that their flag be flown alongside the United States flag, but the U.S. refused. I wrote Ave in February 1960, "The fight is now an old one, whether or not the Panamanian flag should be flown in the Zone and if so, where. . . . Since this is an election year . . . this particular issue has taken on enormous importance. . . . Certain [of the candidates] have blown up the issue to gigantic size hoping to gain popularity from that enormously nationalistic section of voters which is comprised mainly of students (young ones) communists, who see in the issue something which could and really has mixed up most of the internal politics in relation to America which were held by the government."

During riots over the flag issue, the band members were mobilized, given rifles (without ammo), and sent out to look as though we were guarding the part of the fence furthest from the action. We were totally stoned on grass and found it quite amusing, especially when some of the Panamanians we had gotten to know ran up to our area of the fence and asked us where the general was. We (literally) dopily pointed down the line, and they raced off.

The Panamanians had many reasons to rise up, among them the condescending attitude of many Americans stationed there, who acted as though their "hosts" barely existed. Some had never gone into Panama proper; few even tried to learn Spanish; and they shopped at the price-controlled PX. Relations were so bad that in the summer of 1960, a new general initiated what I wrote Ave was "a very self-conscious and totally obvious plan called 'Operation Friendship' and mingling is now greatly lauded. Almost the feeling that 'the more Panamanians you get to your house in the Zone—the quicker your promotion'—or that's the way it seems to me and many of my Panamanian friends. They all feel a bit upset [by] . . . the feeling that they are going out slumming. . . . Sincerity somehow isn't there."

A Place of My Own

THE EVENING BEFORE I left New York for Central America, Chiquita had taken me to the 21 Club for a farewell dinner. The owner, Bob Kriendler, came over to say hello, and Chiq told him where I was heading. I said something like "I don't know what the hell I'm going to do there," and Bob smiled and said, "This is your lucky night, private. You're about to meet some great people." A group of prominent Panamanians were sitting at a table nearby, and Bob brought me over and introduced me. They promised to take good care of me when I got to Panama, and they sure did.

At the first dinner party they invited me to, I met the commanding general of the area. I was wearing my private's uniform, and he said "What are *you* doing here, young man?" I said, "I was invited, sir." He looked at the name tag on my chest, saw "Duchin," apparently made the connection to Dad, and said, "Let's have a little talk after dinner." We found a quiet place, he asked me some questions, then made me a fantastic offer. If I would play at the Officers' Club on Saturday nights, he said, he would arrange for me to live in an apartment in town, where I could come and go freely. The only catch was that I had to be back on base in time for reveille, an agony after a late night. He also explained that, by getting out and around, I would be in an ideal position to gather intelligence and report back to him. In short I would be a "private" eye.

My social life was very odd. I hung out with the richest, most influential people in Panama, among them members of the Arias family. The international lawyer, diplomat, and journalist Roberto Arias, known as "Tito," was married to the prima ballerina Margot Fonteyn. I would see them again in New York and London when Margot and Rudolf Nureyev became magnificent ballet partners.

I also got to know some wonderful artists and intellectuals. At their houses, I would meet Cubans who were highly placed in the Castro organization, stopping off on their way to South America, and we would discuss and argue long into the night. They were mostly young and hip. Some were idealistic members of privileged families, but many were dedicated revolutionaries who had come down from the Sierra Maestra mountains with Castro and been involved in the coup that unseated the corrupt president Fulgencio Batista.

That August, I wrote Ave, "Panama at the moment is quite interesting. . . . Everyone seems to be pondering the meaning of the word revolution, not with the actual action in mind, but more with the ideological concept of Castro's revolution in relation to Latin America or more particularly . . . the Caribbean area, in mind. They believe a precedent has been set, one which will touch off a fuse which stretches through every Latin American country. . . . The frightening aspect . . . is that Communist, pro-Fidel propaganda is rapidly being spread all over the country, even deep into the interior. Pamphlets are often sent to the Cuban Ambassador with only sporadic interference by the Panamanian government. It is a great shame that . . . they do not organize themselves against this danger . . . they just sit back and meditate on the evils of American capitalism and what they suppose to be the evils of Communism."

Ave later told me that he had learned as much from some of my letters as he had from official government reports. I still wasn't sure what I wanted to do when I got out of the Army, and even though a career as a musician seemed almost inevitable, largely because of Averell I'd also been considering working for the State Department. If I was an effective, if unofficial, spy, that might be a good start.

Then I met Cesar Balsa.

A LUCKY ENCOUNTER

IN 1960, CHIQUITA WAS living in Mexico City and asked if I wanted to spend a week with her while I was on leave. I joined her there, and after dinner at a popular restaurant I noticed an unused piano in a corner, walked over, and began to play. It was kind of fun seeing Dad's widow leaning on the piano, enjoying herself. I was in the middle of a tune when a good-looking dark-haired fifty-ish fellow in a pinstriped blue suit walked over. He introduced himself as Cesar Balsa, and told me he owned the restaurant.

"What a terrific kid," he remarked to Chiq. I didn't hear what she said, but she must have told him I was Eddy Duchin's son. "You sound great," he said. "Let's meet in New York when you get out of the Army. By the way, I own the St. Regis hotel."

My response was "Come on, you've got to be kidding." The St. Regis, like the Plaza and the Waldorf, was one of the best and most expensive hotels in New York. He ignored my rude remark, and said, "Hearing you gave me a great idea."

I was discharged later that year, and flew to Newark on the way to pick up my papers. While I was having a beer in the airport with a couple of buddies, the television was on and the Kennedy-Nixon debate was playing. It was the first televised presidential election debate, which was news in itself, and I was riveted. I didn't know it then, but I was witnessing the end of one era and the beginning of another.

THE MAISONETTE

THE KENNEDYS' "CAMELOT" BEWITCHED the country with its charm, talent, and style. Cesar had picked up the new mood, and decided to change the format of the St. Regis nightclub, the Maisonette, to appeal to a chic, younger, attractive, and socially well-connected crowd. His plan was to create a classy supper club for dining and dancing, with a band as the main attraction. He wanted a young bandleader, and because of my father, he thought I might just be what he was looking for.

He would have to compete with the most popular nightclubs and hotel ballrooms in town, among them El Morocco and the Stork Club; the Plaza Hotel's Persian Room; the Waldorf's Starlight Roof and Wedgwood Room; and Rockefeller Center's Rainbow Room. I would eventually play in all of them.

I'd been playing jazz, classical, and Latin music, but at the Maisonette I would have to play "Society music" for the two-step, the waltz, the tango, and more. To master the right tunes and the right tempo, during the summer before the opening I found a job at a briefly hot new nightclub on Long Island. The club attracted the kind of young crowd I hoped would follow me to the Maisonette to dance to the jazzy, relaxed style I was working on. With the help of an experienced musician, I put together a small band, and spent the summer learning Society music.

I'd been to plenty of dances and deb parties, and I knew what the music sounded like, but I hadn't quite gotten a handle on the rhythm. I got up my nerve and called the leading Society bandleader, Meyer Davis. He had known my father, and his career stretched back to my mother's debutante days in the mid-1920s. If anyone could tell me what Society music was, he was the best source.

"I play for rich people all over the country," he said, "and I've found that they have one thing in common. Most of them don't have rhythm, but they can walk, so I play everything at, or close to, march tempo." He hummed a bit of the march tune from the movie *The Bridge on the River Kwai*, and followed it with "It Was Just One of Those Things" in about the same tempo. It was quite amusing to listen to Meyer Davis's version of the "Colonel Bogey March," while I tapped out the rhythm on a table.

September arrived, and as the Maisonette prepared for the opening night, I went back one more time to check that the piano was in tune. The club was located down a flight of red-carpeted stairs, behind a discreetly marked door in the hotel lobby. (When the hotel was built by John Jacob Astor in 1904, the space downstairs was a skating rink.)

Twenty years after Dad died, the most elegant nightclubs had shrunk from the many-chambered Casino to more intimate rooms. Even empty, the redesigned Maisonette was cozy. The walls were covered in red fabric; the banquettes were upholstered in red plush, and gilded wall sconces and little shaded lamps shed a soft, romantic light on the tables. The place wasn't too big, and the dance floor was just the right size. It felt like a place where my band and I would look and feel comfortable.

The first night was a benefit for the International Rescue Committee, chaired by William vanden Heuvel, who later became one of my closest friends; for decades we had lunch at least twice a month. Bill, who died at ninety-one in 2021, was tall and serious-looking, with owl-like glasses, but his sense of humor was matched only by his brilliance. I often played at events where his funny, urbane, and intelligent before- or after-dinner speeches brought an evening or a cause alive.

His most active engagement was as chairman of the Roosevelt Institute. He created Freedom Park at Roosevelt Island in the East River, where I played for the opening party, and on many occasions since. To start the evenings, Bill always sang FDR's theme song, "Happy Days Are Here Again," with great gusto. We joked about his joining the band as a vocalist.

On opening night, my last name attracted important columnists, who were interested to see how well I matched up to Dad; and who could make or break my career in the next morning's papers. Igor Cassini, who wrote a gossip column under the name "Cholly Knickerbocker," which was published in 150 Hearst papers and read by 20 million people; Dorothy Kilgallen; Leonard Lyons; and Earl Wilson were all there. Other guests were friends who had come to cheer me on. I was amazed and proud to have filled the room, but I couldn't help but wonder if the assembled luminaries were there to see and hear me, or if they came for Eddy Duchin's son.

My knees were weak and I was nervous as hell as I smiled, kissed, and shook hands. At last, I sat down at the piano, gave the downbeat, and the newly christened Peter Duchin Orchestra began to play. Our first tune was "Make Someone Happy." My nerves unknotted, and once

I started playing, I never thought of Dad. I was totally focused on the music and the dancers.

Luckily, we got terrific reviews. Many of them mentioned my father, which didn't bother me: I was flattered. After that, the columnists regularly stopped by to check out the room, and often mentioned me.

From then on, nothing in my life was ever the same.

I was on the road to success, but I was still uncomfortable leading musicians who knew a heck of a lot more than I did. From time to time, I'd bring in a star guest, and think "Holy cow! He can play rings around me!" To boost my confidence, I signed up for a class with the famous acting coach Wynn Handman, to help me create the character "Peter Duchin, bandleader." The difference between the way I felt when I started and when I finished studying with Wynn wasn't as much gestures or a pose, but confidence.

Soon the band began to do weekly remote radio broadcasts from the Maisonette, and anyone in the country who had a radio could listen to us and would know who we were. I was establishing a reputation.

The photographer Jerome Zerbe, who was a great friend
of my parents and very helpful when I started at the St. Regis,
documented elegant New York nightlife. Zerbe and two socialites
pose at El Morocco, while another great photographer,
Horst, shoots a photo for a 1938 *Vogue* feature.

Photograph by Horst P. Horst

CHAPTER TEN

Nightclubs,
the Last Dance

The Dreamers

NONE OF THE OWNERS of the Maisonette and its chief rivals, El Morocco and the Stork Club, were New Yorkers. Cesar, of course, was Mexican. El Morocco's handsome John Perona, who looked as though he could have played the natty villain in a movie, with his heavy eyebrows, deep-set eyes that didn't miss much, and the big hands of one of the boxers he followed, was born Giovanni Antonio Perona in Italy. Sherman Billingsley, the Stork Club's proprietor, with his all-American good looks and gangster-riddled past, started as an Oklahoma bootlegger. Each of them wanted to create an incomparably glamorous nightclub.

Perona and Billingsley fashioned environments that reflected their dreams about the most magical city they could imagine. By definition, the best places were exclusive. El Morocco was known to be especially particular about who was admitted, and where they were seated. Billingsley made his point by commissioning a solid gold chain that hung outside the entrance of the Stork Club, where the doorman decided whom to admit.

How did Sherman Billingsley from Oklahoma know who would adorn his club? Like people all over the United States, he read the syndicated gossip columns, and like any ambitious club owner, he courted the columnists, some of whom, like Walter Winchell, would make it "their" club, too.

Cesar's style at the Maisonette was quietly elegant, as befitted the owner of one of the city's most luxurious hotels. Part of my job was to bring that image to life. To illustrate that the hotel, the Maisonette, and I were the essence of glamour, Cesar commissioned the album *Peter Duchin at the St. Regis,* with a sleeve that was meant to show a fresh face, representing a club that didn't need a gold chain to make an impression.

The cover was shot at three in the morning, after hotel porters had hauled a piano onto the sidewalk in front of the hotel. I played, the cameras clicked, and the odd passersby stopped to watch. One man staggered over and asked if he could sit in and play bass, and an attractive woman asked if she could sing with me. The cover did its job, and apparently so did the music: the Maisonette flourished, and I signed on for the next two seasons.

Thinking back on that night, I was reminded of the lyrics in Frank Loesser's song "My Time of Day," one of my favorite tunes from the musical *Guys and Dolls:* "My time of day is the dark time, / a couple of deals before dawn / . . . when the smell of the rain-washed pavement / comes up clean, and fresh and cold / and the streetlamp light fills the gutter with gold." Luckily, the pavement wasn't rain-washed the night of the shoot.

JEROME ZERBE'S EL MOROCCO

EL MOROCCO, KNOWN AS "Elmo's" to insiders, was instantly recognizable in photographs, thousands of which appeared in the gossip columns. The bold navy-blue zebra-striped fabric that covered the banquettes was the background in every picture. (Those who hadn't been to the club assumed the stripes were black, because the photographs were printed in black and white in the newspapers.)

The photographer Jerome Zerbe, who was an old friend of my mother's, was at the club night after night until closing time, snapping pictures of socialites and movie stars for the columnists, who were often in and out of the club to see who was there, and with whom. Readers of the gossip columns feasted on the images; and in 1937, Perona published a book of Zerbe's photographs. I didn't know Dad had played at El Morocco until I looked through the book, but there he was, at the piano. Another photograph shows my parents at a table, celebrating Dad's birthday. Clark Gable's picture occupies the full page next to theirs. I also found a picture of Marie sitting with an unidentified man. I hadn't realized how attractive she was when she was young: the picture was taken long before I was born.

Lucius Beebe, the prolific journalist whose syndicated column, This New York, ran in the *New York Herald Tribune* from the 1930s until 1944, wrote the introduction to Zerbe's book.

"The New York scene was suddenly and in its social entirety taken over by people whose names made news and whose clothes and faces made comparative sense," he noted. Zerbe's El Morocco pictures marked a distinct social change from the time when "Society" preferred to maintain at least a modicum of privacy. Now, Beebe wrote, "the fanciest floor show imaginable to a chic and witty audience of New Yorkers is themselves. . . . That people who enjoy their own company so effusively should also enjoy being photographed and exploited in the public prints doesn't in retrospect seem like such an earth-shaking discovery."

I went to El Morocco from time to time, but I only had one night off a week, and I preferred smaller clubs where pals like Bobby Short or Mabel Mercer were performing: the Blue Angel, or the jazz clubs on 52nd Street and uptown in Harlem, to hear first-rate musicians playing wonderful jazz. In Dad's day, the top Harlem clubs, most famously the Cotton Club, were beautifully appointed and attracted the same kind of folks as the top midtown clubs. The men wore black or white tie, the women were dressed in couture evening gowns. The music was made for dancing, which was livelier than at the clubs downtown, but the greatest difference lay in the performers. The floor shows were famous for their beautiful young women and terrific singers, but while the patrons were White, the performers were Black. Among them were Lena Horne, who started there at the age of sixteen, Ella Fitzgerald, Louis Armstrong, Count Basie, and Billie Holiday.

The Cotton Club had been closed for a while when I went to Harlem. By then, the bands and patrons were integrated, but there were many other clubs that had great jazz, dancing, and performers, and a different kind of energy than Elmo's, the Stork Club, or the Maisonette.

BALLOON NIGHT AT THE STORK CLUB

SHERMAN BILLINGSLEY LEFT HIS native Oklahoma in 1929, after serving a brief jail term in Leavenworth for bootlegging. He arrived in New York, and bought dozens of drugstores, which sold "medicinal liquor" over-the-counter, and stronger brews behind the scenes. He was so successful that a powerful mob leader insisted on owning 30 percent of his business. When Billingsley opened a speakeasy, the deal was the same. In 1931, he was raided by Prohibition agents, but soon reopened on West 51st Street, just off Fifth Avenue. The Volstead Act was repealed two years later and he established the Stork Club in the same location. The mob took a cut there, too. Billingsley tried to become independent, but he didn't make any headway until he was kidnapped and held for ransom by Mad Dog Coll, a rival of his mob partners. The ransom was paid, although it's not clear by whom, and he was freed unharmed. After that, the original gang backed off. If his underworld connections had become public, the club would have lost its cachet.

Billingsley, like Cesar Balsa and John Perona, was determined to attract the cream of café society. Every year, he invited a dozen of the most popular debutantes to be his guests, and as he expected, they attracted their friends. Everything was "on the house" for the girls. They wore Sortilège, the club's exclusive perfume, and tapped their cigarettes in the famous black ashtrays with the Stork Club logo. The ashtrays were such popular souvenirs that Billingsley was constantly buying replacements.

On Sundays, balloons were held above the dance floor in a net that was pulled aside at midnight, when women crowded the dance floor, raising their arms to catch a balloon that might contain a ticket that entitled them to win a hundred-dollar bill, a piece of jewelry, and in one case, the papers for a pedigreed puppy. Some lucky guy even won a Cadillac. It's said that Billingsley's gifts cost the club $100,000 a year, the equivalent of about $855,000 today.

Balloon Night justified my sense that there was something "off" about the place. The Maisonette would never have tried a stunt like that. Yet the club became so prestigious that even Benny Goodman played there. As one author wrote, the Stork Club name was "synonymous with fame, class and money, in no particular order." So much cash poured in that one night, when Ernest Hemingway arrived with a $100,000 check he had received for the movie rights to *For Whom the Bell Tolls,* he asked Billingsley to cash the check—some of the money was probably used to pay off a long-standing tab. Billingsley had enough in the safe to accommodate Hemingway, but said he'd have to wait to collect until closing time at 4:00 a.m.

Favored guests could use the club's private barbershop and its limousine to drive them wherever they wanted to go. The select few were admitted to the Cub Room, an inner sanctum guarded by a maître d' known as "St. Peter," because he decided who was allowed to enter. There, Billingsley and his pals played cards, and Walter Winchell wrote his column and broadcast his nationwide radio show, where, he announced, he was at Table 50. Billingsley's table was Number One.

I rarely went to the Stork Club. It wasn't as much fun as El Morocco, which was more relaxed, and didn't have the gimmicks. Maybe I would have been more interested if I'd known about the gangsters. Now that I think about it, Billingsley's partners were just another version of the mobsters behind the scenes at the Casino.

OVER AND GONE

EL MOROCCO'S JOHN PERONA died in 1961. A few months later, his son sold the club. It reopened in 1964, and the first night attracted such a large crowd that Lee Radziwill had to be turned away, although the Begum Aga Khan was squeezed in. The club was resold a couple of times, and after an incarnation as a steakhouse, opened again in its old form in 1987. *The New York Times* described it as having restored its "full-throttle glamour." The actor Ben Gazzara, who often came to the Maisonette with his wife, Janice, told *The New York Times,* "This place has the one thing missing in my business these days: glamour. It's nice to see it back."

It wasn't back for long. By 1992, El Morocco had closed for good, and the space became a topless bar. The club's first location on 54th Street is now the Citigroup Center; its second, a couple of blocks east, is a condominium.

The Stork Club had a far shorter life. Billingsley refused to allow his workers to join a union and the club was picketed. Patrons didn't want to cross the line; the club lost clients and money; and Billingsley dispensed with the live band. In 1963, he advertised a hamburger and French fries for $1.99. In its heyday, as many as 2,500 guests visited in an evening; in its last months, on some nights fewer than a half-dozen people came in.

He had used all his assets, plus about $10 million

from his three daughters' trust funds, to try to keep the club open, but he finally had to shut it down in 1965. He sold the site to CBS a year before he died; the building was demolished, and the pleasant little Paley Park, named for the father of CBS founder William Paley, now occupies its former location.

Cesar sold the St. Regis to Sheraton Hotels in 1966. The hotel was renamed the St. Regis-Sheraton, and the Maisonette was closed four years after it opened. The only place in the hotel for dining and dancing now is the ballroom on the St. Regis Roof, which is rented for special events.

I loved my gig at the Maisonette, but by the time its day was over, most of my business was private parties. We were enough in demand that whatever the end of the nightclub portended, it didn't affect us financially. The great nightclubs sparkled when every table was taken, the music was terrific, the dance floor was full, and the guests looked rich, attractive, beautifully dressed, tastefully bejeweled, and confident. They conjured a glamour implicit in the décor, the service, the maître d' who greeted the regulars by name, who the guests were and what they wore.

For all that, without music and dancing, the clubs would just have been fancy restaurants (with often mediocre food). The music drew you in as you arrived and enticed you to dance as soon as you'd ordered your first drink. If bandleaders contributed to a sense of glamour, it was because, as the cultural and social historian Virginia Postrel explained, they projected an aura that was "slightly mysterious and somewhat idealized, but not to the extent it is no longer possible to identify with the person." By the end of the 1960s, however, the allure embodied by nightclubs and fine dress and dancing seemed to be on its way out.

DOUBLES, THE LAST OUTPOST

AND YET . . . In 1976, eleven years after the Stork Club closed and El Morocco was in its steakhouse phase, Joe Norban, a successful businessman who had briefly been an investor in El Morocco, opened Doubles, a members-only club downstairs in the Sherry-Netherland hotel.

Norban established a board of socially prominent New Yorkers, who made lists of potential members. In contrast to the Central Park Casino, which was designed as a club until the board of governors discovered that private organizations couldn't be located on city-owned land, Doubles, which was in a hotel, had free rein to choose its policies and its membership.

The entrance is reminiscent of the Maisonette: the discreet lobby door; red-lacquered walls with black-and-white prints by the early-twentieth-century French artist Sem; and cheetah-patterned carpet that leads down to a desk where members check in. The bar is spacious, and the room for dining and dancing is two-tiered, so both spaces feel intimate, and the food is delicious. I played at Doubles on its opening night, and for the next three decades. Disco music has replaced live bands, but I have continued to play there for private parties.

The club's thirtieth anniversary in 2006 was recorded in *Quest* magazine, with an introduction by the then-editor David Patrick Columbia, the social commentator, who later founded and serves as editor-in-chief of the *New York Social Diary*. Columbia wrote that Norban "wanted to create a place to make up for the loss of the great dining and dancing clubs like El Morocco and the Stork Club—a glamorous place where people could meet and greet, and dine and dance. Such venues had all but disappeared from the social map, and it was Mr. Norban's idea that there was still a need for it." Doubles, Columbia wrote, "became the central meeting place for nightlife activity of New York society. It was a club where people could see their friends, but not too broad so that there was that assured sense of exclusivity."

Joe Norban's daughter, Wendy Carduner—dark-haired, trim, stylish, and hardworking—has been the director of Doubles since the late 1980s. The club remains popular for lunch, and busy at night, partly because Carduner has found ways to adapt to changes in society. She explains that one reason for the death of nightclubs like the ones where Dad and I played is the prevalence of the two-job family. When both parents work, they want to spend time with their children in the evenings and go to bed early. To accommodate their lifestyle, Doubles has instituted family nights at Halloween, Christmas, Easter, other occasions during the school year, and popular dance nights for fifth and sixth grade children of members. I can't begin to imagine how five-year-olds, sitting on Santa's lap, would have gone over at El Morocco, but anyway, those days are long gone.

I once had a "date" with Audrey Hepburn. I was in Paris,
on my junior year abroad, and my godmother asked me to pick up
a friend and take her to the opera. Audrey was the "friend."
She was incomparably glamorous, unselfconscious, and made me
feel comfortable right away. As the actor Richard Dreyfuss said,
"She was the kind of dream that you remember when
you wake up smiling."

Photograph by Hulton Deutsch

CHAPTER ELEVEN

Glamour

"I Know It When I See It"

FROM THE TIME I began at the Maisonette, newspapers and magazines persistently described me as "the glamorous Peter Duchin," as if the adjective was part of my name. It sounded pretty shallow to me, but I got used to it, even if I've always thought of myself as anything but glamorous. When I had to wear designer suits for magazine shoots, I felt uncomfortable. I much preferred to be wearing my beat-up waders to fish in a stream.

Glamour and style usually go together, but anyone with taste and money can buy a snappy wardrobe, so what makes a person, an object, or a place seem glamorous?

I asked a friend who had a career as an editor of fashion magazines what she thought about glamour. She asked me why I could possibly be interested. "No one is glamorous anymore," she said. "Anyway, who cares?"

I don't care; I never have; and I agree that glamour, whatever that once meant, has pretty much disappeared. Yet I wanted to understand the atmosphere in which Dad and I succeeded, what people thought they saw in us, and why they imagined that dancing to our music could make them glamorous, too.

The late United States Supreme Court Justice Potter Stewart famously said that pornography is hard to define, "but I know it when I see it." I'd say the same about glamour. It is even more difficult to define, and unlike pornography, the real thing is rare.

The word "glamour," which comes from Scots, means magic and enchantment, and for me, certain kinds of music have those qualities. The art historian Herbert Muschamp was interested in the same magic. In 2005, he wrote a story in *The New York Times Magazine* titled "Playing for Keeps." He focused on me, which I appreciated, but I was really the stand-in for a bigger idea. Muschamp describes the ways in which dance music can create some of the elements I was searching for:

> I know no art more atmospheric than the music of Peter Duchin. . . . The band's . . . specialties are memory and mood . . . the production of feelings under controlled circumstances. The controls are derived from upper-class American etiquette, an association some are put off by . . . [but] I'll take my atmosphere where I can get it . . . the upper crust isn't too low for me. . . .
>
> Duchin's music was as integral to the 1960's as Lou Reed's Velvet Underground. . . . Duchin played at the St. Regis; Reed, on St. Marks Place. But . . . both were featured on the soundtrack of the city, when New York society was opening up.

I agree with Muschamp that music inspires "memory and mood," and as he also wrote, "evaporates into ambience." I'm awfully glad he didn't use the word "glamorous."

MAGIC AND ENCHANTMENT

ANITA LOOS WROTE ABOUT glamour in her very funny autobiography, *A Girl Like I,* published in 1966: "One word, Hollywood, would express the epitome of glamour, sex and sin in their most delectable terms." Anita started her career writing subtitles for the scenes in silent movies, enhancing the illusions with "dialogue" that ran across the bottom of the screen. By the time the talkies came in, she understood how to create an atmosphere with only a few words. She knew how the look, the stance, and the expressions were created, and why the public bought the image. What no one could replicate was the quality the Italians call *sprezzatura,* an absence of any attempt to impress. By definition, anyone who has to try to be glamorous will fail.

I knew I was in the presence of the real thing the first time I saw Marilyn Monroe. She was staying at the apartment of Toots Shor and his wife, "Baby." Marilyn and Joe DiMaggio, who was a buddy of Toots's, were getting divorced, and Toots, the quintessential Damon Runyon New Yorker and the most generous man I've ever known, gave Marilyn a place to stay while the divorce was being negotiated. I was waiting for him to take me to a ballgame when she came downstairs into the living room, where I was sitting. She was wearing a nightgown, which was quite something in itself; but while another beautiful woman in a negligee might have seemed merely sexy, when Marilyn walked in, it was something else. The room changed, the temperature went up, and I sure paid attention.

In 1956, old WASP style had its moment in the sun, as the epitome of glamour. The look, and the life, were portrayed in the madcap romance movie *High Society:* the heroine, Tracy Lord, played by Grace Kelly, speaks with a languid East Coast socialite accent and lives in a quietly elegant house that looks as though it could have been in the same family for a couple of generations.

By 1981, folks like the Lords had been replaced by the Ewings in *Dallas,* the number-one-rated television series. The characters are rich Texans (cattle and oil) who fight about money, power, and who's sleeping with whom. "Glamorous" people are almost always rich, and that's about all the Lords and Ewings had in common.

My friend Larry Hagman played the ruthless oil baron J. R. Ewing. When I stayed with him in Malibu, I discovered that he had a very unusual habit: he never spoke on Sunday. Not a word. He told me that he said quite enough during the week. Some people thought the quirk was amusing; others that it was odd or annoying. His wife, Maj, put up with it; maybe she was glad to have a day off.

Even *Dallas,* with its faux glamour, was out of sync with the times. Among the top movies of 1980 were *The Shining* (horror), *The Empire Strikes Back,* (sci-fi), and *Raging Bull* (boxing, blood and gore). What once seemed glamorous felt trivial in the era that had seen anti-Vietnam activism, and when many people I knew were deeply involved in the civil rights and women's movements.

Despite the change in social climate, my business was doing well, and I was sending musicians to jobs all over the country. Plenty of people still wanted to dance to the kind of music I played, and we also kept up with rock 'n' roll and other hot trends. If I was at the piano, we'd get paid extra.

I've come to believe that the kind of glamour on which I had ridden to success is so ephemeral and outdated as to be virtually meaningless. Good manners are far more important. Yet the social historian Virginia Postrel contends that the *idea* of glamour is timeless. Postrel was only two years old when I started at the Maisonette. By the time she was old enough to go to nightclubs, they were gone. What was she thinking in 2013, when she wrote *The Power of Glamour: Longing and the Art of Visual Persuasion?*

Postrel writes, "The story of glamour is the story of human longing and its cultural manifestations . . . glamour is not trivial."

A "'glamorous' person, setting, or style will not produce glamour unless that object resonates with the audience's aspirations. . . . It depends on maintaining exactly the right relationship between object and audience, imagination and desire. . . . Glamour is fragile because perceptions change."

AUDREY

GLAMOUR DOES EXIST; it can transcend time, and sometimes it's recognizable between cultures, but it involves more than being on the Best Dressed List, a Hollywood star, or a famous entertainer. Few people have it all. Audrey Hepburn did. While perceptions change, it's likely that her magic will not be forgotten anytime soon. She conveyed a dignified modesty, which came through in the roles she played, but was also authentic and very beautiful. Audrey's glamour, as Virginia Postrel might say, was not trivial, and it transcended fads.

I was fortunate enough to experience her magic myself. In fact, she and I once had a "date." When I was living in Paris during my junior year at Yale, my godmother, Ginny Chambers, asked me to pick up a friend, whom she described as a "very attractive woman," and take her to the opera. Ginny gave me the address, but neglected to mention the name of the friend. I arrived at her house, rang the doorbell, and Audrey Hepburn opened the door, wearing an understated black dress and a huge smile. Her smile was nothing compared to mine; I was totally dumbfounded. I said "Are *you* my date?" and she said, "Poor guy, you've got me for the evening."

I was a twenty-one-year-old college boy and Audrey had been a great star since 1953, when the famous director William Wyler cast her in *Roman Holiday* as an oversheltered princess who runs away to see the world, and meets and falls in love with a newspaperman, played by Gregory Peck. The role earned her an Academy Award, as well as Golden Globe and BAFTA awards. She was the first actress to receive all three.

I had seen her in *Sabrina,* playing a sweet young chauffeur's daughter who is sent to finishing school in Paris and returns a beautiful woman, leading the two brothers for whom her father worked (played by Humphrey Bogart and William Holden) to compete for her. That was 1954: I was seventeen and I fell in love with her, too. When I was in Paris, her most recent movie, *Funny Face,* had just come out. She was cast as a shy, intellectual bookstore owner who is discovered by a fashion magazine editor, unwillingly undergoes a makeover as a model, and is sent to Paris to make her début. (Her character comments "Paris is always a good idea," with which I heartily agree.) In one scene she dances with Fred Astaire to songs by George and Ira Gershwin, and keeps up quite well: she was a trained ballerina.

The evening I was Audrey's escort, she quickly made me feel comfortable; she was nice and funny, and knew a lot about opera, so we had plenty to talk about. I've forgotten what was on the stage: what I remember is a beautiful woman who had the grace to find common ground with a college boy so he could forget that he was spending an evening with one of the most famous women in the world.

Her movie image often combined naïveté and fragility with spunk, but she was far from naive. During World War II, living in Holland during the Nazi occupation, she gave underground ballet performances to benefit the resistance, delivered their newspapers, and took food and messages to downed Allied airmen. Food was so scarce that she and her mother ate tulip bulbs and tried to make bread from grass.

When her career was at its peak in 1967, she took a partial break from acting to spend more time with her family. Around then, she was recruited as a Goodwill Ambassador for UNICEF. She said one reason she took the job was that just after the war, she and her mother subsisted on UNICEF care packages. She paid back the organization's generosity by traveling to the poorest places in what she refused to call the "Third World," declaring that we are all "one world." She made the "invisible" visible, through photographs of her in places without clean water, barely any food, the absence of medical care, and where people lived in the most primitive shelters. The conditions, she said, were "not natural disasters but man-made tragedies, for which there is only one man-made solution—peace." She always made it clear that she was only an ambassador, connecting worlds; and that the real work was done by UNICEF—in fact, in Sudan, a water pump was called a UNICEF—but she awakened hundreds of millions of people to what the extremes of poverty looked like.

By then, she was a virtual constellation: the American Film Institute ranked her number three on the list of the "50 Greatest Screen Legends." (Katharine Hepburn was first, followed by Bette Davis; and Elizabeth Taylor was down the list at number thirteen.) Yet she insisted "I never think of myself as an icon. What is in other people's mind is not in my mind. I just do my thing."

Kevyn Aucoin, the makeup artist to the stars, who has seen just about everyone in Hollywood up close, described her as having "an angelic quality. . . . She didn't act like she was better than everyone, she just had a sort of presence, an energy, a sort of light coming from within her that was overwhelming."

Maybe I was wrong to think that glamour is passé; it's just hard to find the real article; those like Audrey, who are truly magical, just do their thing. As she once remarked, "There are certain shades of limelight that can wreck a girl's complexion."

In 1904, my great-great-aunt Tessie Oelrichs gave the "party of the season," a White Ball at Rosecliff, her Newport mansion. The Gilded Age was the beginning of widely publicized, immensely expensive costume parties like the one she was dressed for here. After Rosecliff was donated to the Preservation Society of Newport County, I played at parties in Tessie's magnificent ballroom.

Photograph courtesy of the Preservation Society of Newport County

CHAPTER TWELVE

A Society
Bandleader

MUSICOPHILIA

ANITA LOOS WROTE THAT my mother "Scampered out of the Social Register to marry Eddy Duchin. Today, their son Peter holds the same place as court musician to New York Society as did his father." It's true that I've always been labeled a "Society Bandleader." I love what I do, playing the piano, making people happy, and creating music that makes folks want to dance, but the word "Society" has never sat quite right with me. It's not only arrogant, but it implies that people who have created something of meaning don't count if they don't come from privileged backgrounds.

It helped put "Society" into perspective when I reread *Musicophilia: Tales of Music and the Brain* by the neurologist Oliver Sacks. He writes, the "propensity to music—this 'musicophilia' . . . is manifest and central in every culture, and probably goes back to the beginning of our species. It may be developed or shaped by the cultures we live in, by the circumstances of life, or by the particular gifts or weaknesses we have as individuals—but it lies so deeply in human nature that one is tempted to think of it as innate."

Listening to music, Sacks explains, "is not just auditory and emotional, it is motoric as well. 'We listen to music with our muscles,' as Nietzsche wrote. We keep time to music, involuntarily, even if we are not consciously attending to it, and our faces and postures mirror the 'narrative' of the melody, and the thoughts and feelings it provokes." In short, we dance.

Some anthropologists conjecture that music preceded language. Between 250,000 and 300,000 years ago, even before *Homo sapiens* became hunter-gatherers, they were probably beating sticks or the flats of their hands against hard surfaces, clapping, clicking their tongues, whistling, possibly to mimic bird calls, chanting, and dancing. Their music would have celebrated many of the same kinds of events at which we play: coming of age and mating (deb parties); prayers for good weather (outdoor events); display (money); success in battle (substitute business for battle, and we're back to money); and communication with their gods (weddings).

There we have it: Society music is simply one of the ways to satisfy a basic human instinct, and nearly every social and cultural group has listened to and moved to its own sounds and rhythms. As it happens, the groups my father and I have played for are a subset of society at large. In my case, I should say "subsets," because I've played for many groups with their own kind of music, from Latin to Viennese, rock 'n' roll, rhythm & blues, and at bar mitzvahs and Mardi Gras parties.

"Society"

THE AMERICAN VERSION OF uppercase "S" Society, which led to "Society music" and the "Society bandleader," changed from "landed gentry" in the late nineteenth century to money-denominated status when the accumulation of great industrial and banking fortunes set off a circus of spending. Display reflected the tone of the times and the very rich were happy to show the world what money could buy: mansions, yachts, racing stables, Parisian couture, jewels with royal pedigrees, and anything else they could acquire, including a place in "Society." That's still true today.

For all its implications of old, established families, American Society could be remarkably fluid, at least for those who were White, Christian (but preferably not Catholic), and wealthy. My mother's great-aunt Tessie Oelrichs is the ultimate example of how fast the social world embraced, and still embraces, the newly rich.

Tessie's father, James Graham Fair, was one of the partners in the Comstock Lode, discovered in 1859, and the largest deposit of silver at the time. His wife, Tessie's mother, Teresa Rooney, ran a boardinghouse in Virginia City, Nevada, until James amassed his fortune. With his money behind her, in 1871, she moved into a mansion in San Francisco with her four children, two boys and two girls. Tessie was twelve and her younger sister, Virginia, known as "Birdie," was four in 1883 when Teresa divorced the rough-mannered James for "habitual adultery." She received a large settlement, somehow inserted herself and her daughters into San Francisco Society, and her daughters became eligible "catches."

In 1890, Tessie married Hermann Oelrichs, the well-off U.S. representative of his family's Hamburg-based shipping concern. James Fair was not invited to the wedding, but he gave his daughter $1 million (the current equivalent of about $29 million) to start her off. Four years later, he died at the age of sixty-three, worth an estimated $45 million. He left $40 million (approximately $1.3 billion in 2021), in trust to Tessie and the beautiful Birdie, who married William Kissam Vanderbilt II in 1899.

The sisters proceeded to Newport, where Tessie would become one of the guardians of the summer colony's social gate. She commissioned Stanford White to build her a $2.5 million mansion modeled after Louis XIV's seventeenth-century Grand Trianon; and fittingly named it Rosecliff: it was on a magnificent site with a view of the sea; and the prior owners had created a famous rose garden.

TESSIE'S "PARTY OF THE SEASON," NEWPORT, 1904

TESSIE'S TRIUMPH WAS HER 1904 "Ball Blanc" aka "White Ball" (in the Gilded Age, knowing French was considered a sign of "good breeding"). She asked the officer in charge of the Newport naval station to lend her a selection of white ships to be anchored where they could be admired from her balconies. When he declined to accommodate her, she created her own naval honor guard, a fleet of faux ships painted white. The drama didn't stop there: the driveway, grounds, terraces, and house were lit with 2,500 white electric lights, at a time when only 3 percent of all homes in the United States were electrified.

Everyone at the ball, including the waiters, was dressed in white, although some men ignored the instructions and wore black tie. Tessie's gown was made of elaborate hand-made lace, which at the time was as expensive as emeralds.

Her pearls fell to her waist, and her hair was topped with an ostrich plume and decorated with diamonds and pearls. Maybe the plume referred to the headpiece young English women wore when they were introduced to the monarch.

The *Newport Daily News* described the White Ball as "the event of the season." My grandmother Marjorie, who was twenty-one that year, was almost certainly among the guests.

Tessie died in 1926, and Rosecliff was sold, then sold again. In 1971, the last private owners donated the house and its furnishings, along with $2 million for its maintenance, to the Preservation Society of Newport County, and it became a tourist attraction.

The house is rented for weddings, parties, and charitable events and I've often played in my great-great-aunt's cream-paneled and gilded ballroom. At 40' x 80', it's only a few inches smaller than the Grand Ballroom at the Plaza. In Tessie's day, a grand organ was installed at one end of the room, but by the time I came along it had been removed and replaced by a gold piano.

Once, as my band was setting up, a janitor approached me and said, "Mr. Duchin, I've been wanting to meet you. We have a children's saddle in the basement, and I always wondered if it was yours." I didn't want to dash his hopes by telling him I hadn't been born when the saddle was used.

I've noticed that at Rosecliff and other grand historic houses, the guests often adjust their behavior to suit the surroundings: their comportment is more formal and they're more conscious of the way they look and act than in other settings. I've often played at the White House, where people are generally on their best behavior; but great mansions also inspire a certain decorum. In more recent years, even at formal parties in hotel ballrooms, when I look out from the bandstand, I often see little rectangles of light, as people turn away from their dinner partners to talk on their cell phones, check their messages, or send texts. Just one look at Tessie's ballroom is enough to tell you that sort of manners would spoil the effect.

SOCIETY ANIMALS

THE NEWPORT SUMMER SEASON was so crammed with fancy dinners and balls that, in order to outdo each other and avoid ennui, hostesses came up with exotic themes. The sour-faced, viper-tongued Mamie (Mrs. Stuyvesant) Fish, who ruled the resort along with Tessie and Alva (Mrs. Oliver) Belmont, was prone to featuring animals. Mamie gave one dinner for her dog, who arrived wearing a $10,000 diamond collar, and another for a "prince," who turned out to be a dressed-up monkey. The little creature was "over-served" with Champagne, and enlivened the evening by swinging on the chandeliers and throwing light bulbs at the guests. Mamie's imagination was extensive, if impractical. One night she hired an elephant, and gave the guests bags of peanuts to feed him as they danced by, trying to avoid the steaming piles the poor beast occasionally dropped. Elephants, by the way, dance to music. I doubt that one was in the mood.

Animal, avian, and lepidopteran themes were popular, if not always successful Gilded Age diversions, and not only in Newport. A Philadelphia family imported ten thousand colorful butterflies from Brazil for their daughter's debutante party. The butterflies were hung from the ballroom ceiling in muslin bags, and were to be released at midnight. Unfortunately, they were asphyxiated, and the guests were pelted with dead insects.

Ward McAllister, whose life was organized around Society and parties, arranged for a thirty-foot "pond" to run the length of his dining room table, and borrowed four swans from the Brooklyn Botanical Garden to paddle around gracefully during dinner. Instead, the birds fought, splashed, and made shrieks and raspy cries. Fortunately for the guests, if not for the swans, they were confined inside a ceiling-high gold wire netting cage; swans are notably aggressive, and when riled are inclined to attack.

The animal world has also occasionally been a feature of our gigs. During a benefit at the New York Bronx Zoo, a concerned animal lover asked me to keep the volume down, in case the noise upset the giraffes. I've forgotten if we muted the sound, but I suppose we might have. At the Richmond, Virginia, zoo, a costumed animal trainer appeared with a heavily sedated lion. The trainer asked me if it was okay for the lion to jump on the piano. I told him it was probably fine; the poor fellow was far too stoned to be dangerous, but he had terrible breath.

On another evening, a gorgeous woman came over and asked if she could sit on the bench next to me. I said sure; she sat, and I saw that a very large mottled snake was draped around her neck and shoulders. That was a bit unsettling, but I kept on playing. The woman thanked me: "Henry" (I think that was the reptile's name), she said, "loves music."

Dogs are often featured at parties to raise money for animal welfare causes. I've played for the ASPCA, and for ARF, an animal rescue organization in East Hampton, Long Island, which cares for dogs and cats, and seeks loving homes for them. While I play "How Much Is That Doggie in the Window", handlers march homeless dogs across a stage in the hope that they will be adopted. Some of them always are.

The pampered poodle Cornelius was something else. I was asked to bring a trio to a small party at a restaurant in Palm Beach, only to discover that we would be playing for five people and a dog. In preparation for the gig, my vocalist and guitar player, Roberta Fabiano, had recorded the sound of barking. From time to time, she turned on the barks and Cornelius leapt off his seat at the table, raced to the speaker, and barked right back. At dinner, I was invited to join the hosts. I was seated next to Cornelius, who had his own place card. He wasn't interested in the first course, which was some kind of seafood, but he neatly devoured the steak, and his manners were quite good. It was his birthday, but I don't recall whether the cake had his name spelled out in icing.

Louis Auchincloss, lawyer, author, and unapologetic snob, wrote incisively of "the social-climbing insider trader in the film *Wall Street,* [who was] seeking the prestige of membership on the board of the Bronx Zoo. [He] remarks that WASPs don't like people, but they 'sure as hell like animals.'"

THE SOCIAL REGISTER

A SYMBOL OF BELONGING to Society, depending on whom you ask, was inclusion in *The Social Register*. A private subscription-only book founded in 1887, it lists "socially important" families, along with their addresses, schools, and clubs, abbreviated for space. (The assumption is that anyone in the book will know that "T" stands for the Tuxedo Club.) My grandmother's family, the Turnbulls, were in the first edition, but after my mother married Dad and was dropped, she told the gossip-hungry press, "So what? It's only a phone book." The family ban is evidently still in place: I've never been listed, which is fine with me.

Another indication of being in the right set was inclusion in *Town & Country,* which began photographing social personalities around 1901. The magazine celebrated its 150th anniversary in 1996 with a two-volume publication, packed in a slipcase. One of the books, *High Society: The Town & Country Picture Album, 1846–1996,* opens with an essay that describes the magazine in its early days as "society's weekly family album, filled with informal photographs of the rich and the wellborn at play."

Well into the 1970s, that still wasn't far off the mark. Slim Aarons, the famous Society photographer, described his subjects as "Attractive people, doing attractive things in attractive places." His iconic full-color photographs depict a sun-filled life, when leisure, at least for the rich, was in plentiful supply.

Times change: take a look at *T&C* today: the Society women who were displayed on nearly every cover have largely been supplanted by entertainment stars, who are, of course, also extraordinarily privileged, and very rich.

SOCIETY MUSIC

ARTICLES ABOUT IMPORTANT GILDED Age parties went into excruciating detail, but the bandleaders were almost never mentioned. Until the 1920s, bands were no more than the servants of the dance, or background music. One newspaper report about a grand party in New York was typical: the writer left out the name of the band, but described its location: out of sight, behind a screen of roses and thorny smilax, known as the carrion vine because of its unpleasant smell.

Name bands became nationally famous in the 1930s, with the growth of radio. In the early days, Big Band broadcasts dominated the airwaves, and featured Dad and other great bandleaders, including Benny Goodman, Glenn Miller, the Dorsey Brothers, Duke Ellington, Guy Lombardo, Louis Armstrong, and Count Basie. Bands traveled from city to city; local newspapers published their schedules, and posters were hung outside large ballrooms to announce the upcoming attractions.

Among Dad's gigs was the tony Glen Island Casino in New Rochelle, New York, with its 60' x 124' main room, where guests wore white tie and tails and evening gowns. At the less dressy Roseland Ballroom in Manhattan, the floor was big enough for 2,500 people to dance at once.

Some bands had commercial sponsors, and record companies backed top bands, which spread their fame even more widely.

During Dad's career the Big Bands were a national phenomenon; and when I began at the Maisonette the trend continued. Both of us have played tunes from the Great American Songbook, which have passed the test of time, starting in the late 1900s, and continuing today, as they will tomorrow. Even now, folks who might not know the names of the composers are likely to recognize "'S Wonderful," "Night and Day," or "Blue Skies," and get up and dance.

The influence of Big Band and Society music has unmistakably waned, but there is still an appetite for formal parties. Today, folks are as likely to dance to the kind of music we played half a century ago, as they are to tunes like Aretha Franklin's "Respect," which always fills the floor. I've come to take it for granted at those parties that the rooms won't be filled with cigarette smoke; but another welcome difference is more subtle: the guests cover a far broader spectrum of society, and by that I don't mean "Society."

Sally Johnson's beautiful coming-out dance at her parents' home
on Lookout Mountain, Tennessee, was the first of the many terrific
parties that earned me the nickname of "The Debs' Delight."

Photograph courtesy of Sally Johnson Shy

CHAPTER THIRTEEN

"The
Debs' Delight"

SALLY'S PARTY

MY REPUTATION AS A society bandleader began in 1963, when I was hired to play at the first of the many debutante parties and cotillions that became an important part of my early business. It didn't take long for me to be described as "The Debs' Delight." My friends often kidded me about that, and called me "Duch, the DD."

Not quite four months into my first season at the Maisonette, Sally Johnson, a lively, pretty blonde from Tennessee, came to New York to be presented at a couple of debutante balls. The following June, she would have her own party at her family's house, and they hadn't settled on a band.

Sally and her parents were staying at the Plaza, only a couple of blocks from the St. Regis, and one night they decided to stop by the Maisonette. They were walking down the stairs when Sally heard the music, and told her parents, *"That's* the band I want at my party." Her father, who played the piano, and her mother, a graduate of the Juilliard School of Music, also liked what they heard. By the end of their stay in New York, they had spent many evenings dining and dancing in that red room; we had gotten to know each other, and I was booked for Sally's party.

That June, the Johnsons invited me to stay at their

house on Lookout Mountain, which overlooks seven states; and Sally and her father showed me the Tennessee Valley from their boat. They gave me the principal guest room, where the prize piece of furniture was an antique bed that had belonged to a distinguished ancestor. The bed collapsed in the middle of the night. I slept on the floor.

The dance began at 9:00, after preliminary dinners at friends' houses. Guests were ushered down the terrace steps to a formal Italianate garden designed for the party. The tent was pink, so was the dance floor, and the tent poles were twined with roses. Sally, her parents, grandparents, and older sister stood in a receiving line to greet their five hundred guests. By the time we started to play, people were already having a good time. Neighbors all over the valley opened their windows to hear the music.

Deb parties often lasted until dawn, and hosts served a light supper around midnight: at the Johnsons', biscuits, country ham, and scrambled eggs were meant to sop up the liquor many of the boys drank from their fathers' silver flasks. On the way to the terrace, waiters led the guests up the stairs in the bunny hop.

Sally and I are still friends, and she says that the high point of the party for her was a song titled "Sally," which I wrote with my second pianist Hal Turner. The lyrics began "Clouds may come and by and by rains may come from out the sky / but Sally makes the day seem sunny . . ." and leads to the penultimate assertion that Sally will be "mine to love and adore . . ." The band played on, and I led Sally in a dance. After the party, Mr. Johnson ordered 250 music boxes that played the tune, and gave them to friends.

The only other song I ever wrote for a party was for Luci Johnson's wedding reception at the White House.

COTILLIONS

MANY OF MY JOBS, especially between the mid-1960s and around 1990, were for debutante cotillions. In New York, the dances were often held at the St. Regis Roof or the Plaza's Grand Ballroom. Sometimes I was asked to send my bill to the debutantes' grandparents, especially if the grandmothers had come out at the same cotillions, and were passing along the tradition. In and around New York as late as the 1970s, debutantes were still symbolic of an exclusive world. Even *The New York Times* published their portraits, with brief articles listing the names of their parents; sometimes their ancestors; where they went to school; and which balls they would be attending.

The cotillions usually followed the same routine: each girl was escorted by one or two boys, or by her father. The men wore white tie and tails or dinner jackets, while the debs wore white dresses and fine kid gloves that reached over their elbows. The hands of the gloves could be unbuttoned and turned back for midnight supper. The ratio of boys to girls was critical. To give each debutante the chance to meet as many boys as possible, and be sure there weren't any wallflowers, the cotillion committee invited extra boys to fill the "stag line," young men who stood around the edge of the dance floor, waiting to cut in.

The boys weren't necessarily interested in dancing. Often, they drank to mute boredom, or overcome shyness.

One boy was known to pack a couple of pieces of toast in the little pocket in the back of his tails, which was designed to hold his gloves. His theory was that the toast would sop up the liquor he was drinking and keep him relatively sober. It didn't. I saw him on the dance floor at quite a few parties, and pitied his partners: he whirled them around until they were ready to stumble, and sometimes they did.

One of my favorite deb parties is the one that didn't happen. The chairman of an international corporation had already sent me the deposit for his daughter's coming-out party when I got a call from him. He told me that his daughter had asked him to spend the money on a charitable cause, rather than on an expensive party. He said he was proud of her. He didn't want his deposit back, but I gladly refunded it.

Parties are not social events for me; they're business, no matter how well I know the hosts. I've always been interested in helping to create a successful evening, and at the height of the debutante flurry, I didn't really think about how tightly and narrowly the tradition was woven into the social fiber. The money was coming in and my career was thriving. Now as I consider those times, the mild and the wild, I feel as though they had taken place in another world, even though the parties continue in full force in certain towns, many of them in the South.

In 2013, *New York Social Diary*'s David Patrick Columbia commented, "the image of the debutante [has] become a media circus of both young women and men pursuing publicity and branding rather than marital alliances. . . .

Young women . . . expect to advance themselves through education and careers, rather than marriage. . . . They also live in a world where the word 'marketing' . . . is a key to accomplishment and achievement. . . . What has changed is the world—changed to suit the debutantes, the young woman of tomorrow."

"Tomorrow" came a long time ago for some young women. In 1925, a year after my mother's debutante season, she dismissed the idea that a deb's singular goal was to nab what was referred to as "a ring by spring." At the same time, her friend and fellow post-deb Ellin Mackay granted an interview to the New York *Daily News*. Ellin explained, "The society girl today is far more independent than her mother and her aunts were, which is a hopeful symptom in the younger generation . . . a girl who can be a success as a debutante in New York society . . . can hold her own later on in most anything she undertakes."

She was challenged to "hold her own" a year later, when she married the great composer Irving Berlin, a Russian Jewish immigrant. Her recently rich and socially ambitious father, Clarence Mackay, disinherited her. They were reconciled after the stock market crash destroyed his fortune, and Mackay had to move out of his mansion, into the superintendent's house on his property. The royalties from just one of Berlin's tunes, "Always," would have been enough to provide Mackay with a comfortable life, but he managed to get along without his son-in-law's help. Ellin and Irving were married for sixty-two years, and had three children.

NIGHTS TO REMEMBER

I'VE MADE MY CAREER playing at big parties, but when I'm not working, I often like small dinners, where guests can relax in private. One of my most indelible memories was the night the publisher Bennett Cerf and his wife, Phyllis, gave a dinner at their country house. I wasn't there to provide the music, but the Cerfs had a piano, and when Walter Cronkite arrived, he quietly gestured to me to step aside. He wanted to know if I would play "The Stripper" later in the evening. "Sure," I said, "but why?" He smiled under his neat mustache and said, "It's a surprise."

After dessert, the group moved into the living room for coffee; I sat down at the piano; and Walter went upstairs. He whistled when he was ready, and I began to play, as he slowly descended, making exaggerated stripping gestures. He started by pulling off his tie and ended in his boxer shorts. There was "the most trusted man on television," wearing blue boxers and dangling a sock from one hand. We were all still laughing after Walter finished his show. Frank Sinatra was there that night, and he was doubled over in hysterics. Frank was a great performer and a good friend, but I don't think he ever tried a stunt like that.

Larger private parties can also provide interesting surprises. I'm thinking about a dance in Venice, which my friend Giovanni Volpi held in a Grand Canal palazzo that had been in his family for centuries. The guest of honor was one of his cousins, who claimed to be the queen of Italy. Although Italy has been a republic since 1946, she was treated with great respect. It was quite a special evening; some of the guests had come from England, other European countries, and the United States.

I always scan the dance floor while I'm playing, and often pick up little vignettes that aren't necessarily meant to be seen. That night I noticed that a Brit whom I knew quite well, and whose wife I liked very much, was dancing in a very sexy way with a famously sexy woman. During a break he came over and asked if I knew her, then lowered his voice and told me that he had made a date to see her the next day. What did I think?

What I thought was that, even though he was a friend, I wasn't going to help him betray his wife, so I made up the first story that came to mind. Maybe the ghost of one of the bloody Borgias inspired me: I told him that she certainly was attractive, but he might want to know that she was said to have stalked her prior husband and tried to hit his new wife in the head with her evening bag when they accidentally met up in the ladies' room one night. "Of course, that's only a rumor," I said, "but a lot of people believe it."

Giovanni had told me not to stop "until the end," which turned out to be six in the morning, when I played "The Party's Over," and Giovanni said, "Okay, let's go home." I was staying with him and his girlfriend at his other house, a villa on the Giudecca, the island in the Venetian lagoon, which is famous for Palladio's Church of the Redentore.

As we were ready to depart in Giovanni's handsome old wood Chris-Craft, the beautiful girl took off her shoes, dropped them into the boat, and stood there for a moment with her long dress blowing in a little puff of air. We shed our jackets and ties; our evening shirts were damp with sweat, and as the boat passed down the Grand Canal into the lagoon, we pulled the shirts away from our skin and flapped them, until the breeze cooled us off. It had been dark when we set out, but soon the light began to come up, an oyster gray, melting into a pale rose, shining on the water. We could see St. Mark's Square and the Chiesa della Salute, the Palazzo Ducale, and the Church of San Giorgio emerging into the soft day as we approached the island.

In my bedroom at Giovanni's villa, I went to the window to close the blinds before I lay down to sleep, and heard a man way out on the lagoon, practicing jazz on his saxophone. It was pure magic.

Truman Capote was at the height of his fame when he gave his
famous masked Black and White Ball. The guest of honor was
Katharine Graham, above, publisher of *The Washington Post.*
Truman bought himself a cheap black mask, but took it—and his
glasses—off for the photographers.

Photograph by Santiago Visalia

CHAPTER FOURTEEN

Truman Capote's
"Party of the Century"

The Black and White Ball

TRUMAN CAPOTE'S VOICE, BETWEEN a squeak and an embedded Southern drawl, was as distinctive as his petite size, his full larder of gossip, and his unique talent. The day in 1965 when he called me and announced "Peter? This is Tru" in his unmistakable voice, it was pretty clear who was on the other end of the line.

I was a big fan, but I didn't know him well enough to call him "Tru," and I figured he had an agenda. We had only met at George Plimpton's literary-packed evenings, and at a dinner at Bill and Babe Paley's, and he certainly hadn't come to the Maisonette to dance.

Truman was calling, *in the strictest confidence* he said at least three times, to discuss the Black and White dance he was planning to give at the Plaza Hotel.

He asked me if I was free and if I wanted to play. I was a young, fresh face; I'd recently been featured on the cover of *Town & Country;* and I knew a lot of the people he was going to invite. As Deborah Davis explains in her delightful and insightful book *Party of the Century: The Fabulous Story of Truman Capote and His Black and White Ball,* "It wasn't just about Peter's talent; it was the fact that he was one of them. Even the music had to come from somebody who could be a guest."

It was obviously going to be a great gig, with terrific publicity for the band: Truman was a brilliant self-publicist, and I knew—*everyone* knew—that he was aiming to give "the party of the century." I was flattered that he'd thought of me, told him so, and said we'd have a hell of a party. We agreed on a price somewhat below my normal fee; and he swore me to secrecy again, chirping, "No one must discover who is on the guest list until the invitations go out, and I don't want anyone to know the least little details." The day after I spoke to him, I began to get calls from columnists saying, "I hear you're playing for the party." So much for secrecy. The charade kind of amused me.

To create a raison d'être, Truman decided he needed an honoree other than himself. He chose Katharine Graham, the publisher of *The Washington Post* and *Newsweek*. Her husband, Phil, had committed suicide in 1963 at the age of forty-eight. Phil had been the publisher of the *Post,* and Kay had taken over his role. She was learning on the job, and still in mourning. Truman told her he was giving the party "to cheer her up."

A catty rumor circulated that he barely knew Kay; but in fact, they were friends. They had met when they joined Gianni and Marella Agnelli cruising the Mediterranean on a supremely luxurious yacht. Later, Truman organized a trip to New York and Washington for couples from Kansas who had helped him when he was writing his masterpiece, *In Cold Blood.* Kay gave a party for them, and invited some of the most distinguished people in government and society to attend.

A more likely honoree might have been one, or all, of the Society women he cultivated, who confided in him over daily lunches at the Côte Basque or the Colony. His special friends included Babe Paley, Gloria Guinness, C. Z. Guest, Marella Agnelli, Slim Keith, and the two princesses: Lee Radziwill and Luciana Pignatelli. They were all beautiful, stylish, rich (or married to rich men), admired, and constantly photographed. He was invited to their dinner parties and country house weekends, and he must have been a terrific guest because he was so clever and, when the mood struck, apt to shock. And, of course, he was a brilliant writer.

The members of his coterie were regulars on the annual Best Dressed List, which was widely published in magazines and newspapers. Babe Paley was number one so often that she was elevated to the Hall of Fame to give someone else a chance. Her beautiful daughter, Amanda Burden, the socially impeccable epitome of youthful style, was next in line. (Amanda outgrew the socialite category. She earned a master's degree in City Planning; served as the New York City planning commissioner; and is now a principal at Bloomberg Associates, one of Michael Bloomberg's philanthropic initiatives, which works with local governments to help them improve the quality of life in their cities.)

If Truman were to choose one of the women in his intimate group as the guest of honor, the others would be mortally offended; and if he wanted his party to make news, he needed someone with stature. Kay had no social ambitions and little if any interest in high style, but she was more powerful than all the others combined.

A PUBLICITY HIGH

IN 1965, *In Cold Blood* had been on the best-seller list for sixteen weeks. A paperback version was coming out soon and would have the largest first print run of any paperback to date. That December, the dramatization of Truman's short story *A Christmas Memory* would be aired on ABC. The Broadway version of *Breakfast at Tiffany's,* renamed *Holly Golightly,* was scheduled to open on December 26; and the movie of *In Cold Blood* was in the works.

Truman was at the peak of his career, from which, of course, there is nowhere to go but down. But for him, nothing was ever enough.

He talked about the party so incessantly that Cecil Beaton wrote in his diary, "What is Truman trying to prove? The foolishness of spending so much time organizing a party is something for a younger man, or a worthless woman to indulge in, if they have social ambitions."

The lead-up was enmeshed in a fever of anxious speculation about who would and wouldn't be invited. Friends and acquaintances courted him. The old-fashioned black-and-white school notebook, which he obsessively guarded, and in which he obsessively added and deleted names in his tiny scratchy handwriting, became the artifact of the season. He was rarely seen without it.

Truman elevated his dance to "The Party of the Century" through his publicity wizardry. He dangled information in front of columnists, as if they were hyenas, waiting for red meat. Several of them had gone so far as to ask me if I would smuggle them in as part of the band. Of course I said no.

To put himself over the top, he cast his party as a social engineering experiment: he would invite people who didn't usually meet outside of their own circles. The invitation list would include folks from old-name and nouveau Society; artists and writers; Hollywood stars; and friends he'd made in Kansas when he was writing *In Cold Blood.* The Kansans were bankers, lawyers, and successful businessmen, but it was doubtful that they would know the other guests. One of the party's distinctions, he later claimed, was that he was the first high-profile host to blend socialites, artists, writers and publishers, advisors to presidents, movie stars and entertainers at a major ball. Considering their 1946 party in Hollywood, I imagine that Dad, Cary Grant, Jimmy Stewart, and John McClain would have disagreed.

NOVEMBER 28, 1966

TRUMAN'S COVETED INVITATIONS ARRIVED at last, or for the unlucky, they didn't arrive at all. The specified attire was black and white, with masks and fans. A frenzy erupted as women competed to commission the most original, gorgeous, and expensive masks. Some were made in Paris, others by such hot haberdashers and later designers as Halston and Adolfo. The extravagant concoctions would festoon the party, which relieved Truman of the need to spend a fortune decorating the Plaza's Grand Ballroom.

On that rainy night four days after Thanksgiving, I dressed in my tuxedo, tucked a white carnation into my buttonhole, and went into the nursery to give Jason, our first child, a kiss. Then I settled him in his crib and told his nurse that Cheray and I would be home late. Cheray was wearing a beautiful headdress meant to resemble a swan, with a perfect plume of white feathers, tucked wings, and a feathery mask. I wonder whether Jason was frightened or fascinated to see his mother transformed into a bird.

I arrived early to set up the band. Truman's promotion had paid off: hundreds of photographers were massed outside the hotel and in the lobby as the ballroom filled with famous people; a few carefully selected gossip columnists; and a battery of security men, wearing evening clothes and simple black masks so they would fit in—and we started to play.

The masks were meant to add a frisson of mystery, but vanity often prevailed. Nearly all the guests wanted their pictures taken, and scarcely anyone took the private elevator. The party gave rise to a new kind of reportage: CBS did its first live coverage from the ball. The photographers were inexperienced in shooting that kind of event, and as Deborah Davis reports in *Party of the Century,* "Half the time the camera is photographing people's feet, but the actual broadcast was a little better. It bridged old-fashioned coverage and something new."

Few beauties were eager to hide their faces. One stand-out was Luciana Pignatelli, who wore a sixty-carat diamond borrowed from Harry Winston on her forehead. The heavy jewel was suspended with some kind of device inside an exaggerated beehive hairdo, topped with a high swoop of feathers. She was accompanied by two body-guards from Winston's. I was told they even followed her into the ladies' room.

Truman made his own understatement: he wore a thirty-nine-cent black Lone Ranger mask from the toy store F.A.O. Schwarz, and gave me an identical one.

The headdresses and such remind me of a story the great photographer Horst told me about Diana Vreeland, when she was the editor of *Vogue*. She was sending him to the Soviet Union for a photo shoot, and he asked what she was looking for. In her raspy, upper-class voice, she drawled "Bring me *splendour!*" That night in the Plaza's gilded ballroom, the astonishing array of feathers, glitter, and jewels worn by some of the most beautiful women in the world was pretty splendid.

I played signature songs written by some of the guests, or made famous by such others as Frank Sinatra, who was the evening's biggest star. The waiters were particularly thrilled to see him, and not only because he was a lavish tipper—he gave his waiter a hundred dollars; the man told me he was going to frame the bill.

The party was really jumping; and I caught a glimpse of the two tallest men in the room, George Plimpton (6'4") and the famous economist John Kenneth Galbraith (6'9"), standing up, tossing each other a roll wrapped in a napkin.

Deborah Davis kindly describes the music as "intoxicating." She didn't mean that the guests were drunk, although some of them were, but I was happy that the dance floor was jammed all night.

The evening also led to an interesting one-night stand. To be sure there would be plenty of men to dance with unaccompanied women, Truman had invited an assortment of single men who would look well in a dinner jacket. The sixty-four-year-old Tallulah Bankhead spent much of the evening with a handsome younger man, whom she took home. In the morning, she called Truman to find out who "that divine man" was. "My doorman," Truman said.

When people ask me about Truman's dance, I have to admit that, except for the excitement it stirred up, the party wasn't much different from others at which we've played. Deborah Davis explains why the party has become legend.

It "was branded from the inception," she explained, "a publicity event, staged brilliantly from start to finish. And yes, the party did not inspire people from different worlds to start hanging out with each other. But it did launch the idea and open the gates by very publicly raising the question, why can't these disparate groups mix in a social meritocracy? A hot magazine editor who came from 'nowhere' was bound to be more interesting than someone who just had an old name. Whatever happened that night, the concept was a template for what followed."

That may be true, but Truman's attempt to mix people from different groups was more idea than reality. His companion Jack Dunphy observed, as Davis recounted, "I've never seen such ghettoizing in all my life. . . . No group mixed with another group."

The Black and White Ball had a huge influence on my career. The logic was that "Peter Duchin played at Truman Capote's famous Black and White Ball. If I hire him, he'll make *my* party (and me) special, too." Hosts who would never see a sixty-carat diamond or a mask that cost thousands of dollars fed on the widely disseminated images of the ball, and half a century later Black and White themes are still popular. I've played at more than I can count, as recently as the summer of 2019. Deborah Davis estimates that she has been invited to at least ninety "Black and White Balls" since her book was published in 2006.

Curiously, for the most part it's more the theme than the memory of the host that has lingered, outside of a relatively small and shrinking group. A Google search turns up pages of ads for decorations with titles like "Black and White Ball—So Lets [*sic*] Party."

Maybe it had something to do with Truman's desperate attempt to "be the start of something big," as the song goes, but after that I became increasingly doubtful about the effect of highly publicized parties on their hosts' status. As one publication wrote, "Peter Duchin seems to be taking a dimmer view of the social whirl of the jet set. 'Those who are susceptible to society crap are not going to be taken that seriously. . . . I don't think going to a lot of fancy parties is good for you.' . . . He expressed some doubt . . . that associating with the Beautiful People had helped his friend Truman Capote, for whose celebrated masked ball he had supplied the music."

I helped my friend, the gossip columnist Igor Cassini find a DJ for Le Club, the first stylish disco in New York. I couldn't imagine why anyone would go out to dance to records they could play at home, instead of to a live band. Boy, was I wrong!

Photograph by Hal Buksbaum

CHAPTER FIFTEEN

The Discotheque
Revolution

Dancing to Records?

IT NEVER OCCURRED TO me that my Panamanian friend Slim Hyatt might turn out to be a star DJ, or that spinning records could become a replacement for live music. Instead, through Slim, I helped to start the discotheque craze in New York, which would deeply encroach on my business. Seeing and hearing live musicians playing in real time was, to me, so much more exciting than listening to someone play records, which anyone could do at home. I simply couldn't imagine that the fad would catch on.

I hardly need to report that I was wrong, and although, even as electronic music has become extremely sophisticated, I still far prefer to hear and see musicians at work.

The disco revolution began in Paris in 1958, the year that Régine Zylberberg, the self-described "Queen of the Night," opened Régine's in Paris. A few years later, an Old Etonian, Mark Birley, established Annabel's, a members-only club in London, named after his wife, the daughter of the Marquess of Londonderry. Annabel's was so exclusive that the younger royals came there to dine and dance.

The first classy discotheque in Manhattan was Le Club, opened in 1960 by Olivier Coquelin, a Frenchman living in New York, in partnership with Igor Cassini, known to his friends as Ghighi. As part of the "jet set,"

Ghighi knew he could attract an exclusive international membership, and he did: according to *The New York Times,* when Le Club got going, it had six hundred resident members and six hundred nonresidents, who included thirteen princes, thirteen counts, four barons, three princesses, and two dukes. The quietly anonymous awning was in place; so was the brass plaque reading "Members Only," and the wood-paneled room was decorated. All that was missing was a DJ, and Ghighi called me to ask if I had any ideas.

The only person I could think of was Slim. He didn't have any experience as a DJ, but as far as I (or Ghighi) knew, neither did anyone else of note. Technically, the job was pretty simple: spinning records. The trick was to have a wide range of dance music, know what to play and when to play it, keep an eye on the dance floor, and create a mood that suited the crowd.

I suggested that the two meet; Slim passed the "test," whatever that involved, and Ghighi hired him. Le Club became the most popular and selective nightclub in town, and Slim became the first celebrity disc jockey in New York. He was soon so heavily booked for parties that it was difficult to get on his schedule.

Discotheques were already gaining traction when Le Club opened, and within a few years, disco music became nearly universal. Now, DJs even follow us at parties. My band plays during the first part of the evening; then, around the time dessert is served, a DJ takes over, the decibel levels soar, and the dancing becomes frantic and free-form.

That's when I leave.

THE DIGITAL SOUND

I'VE ALWAYS BEEN PUZZLED by the sheer volume of disco music, which has become increasingly amplified by high-intensity sound systems that play at a level live musicians can't achieve. I decided that instead of complaining about the noise, I'd find out a little more.

I asked New York University professor Dan Freeman, who began as a jazz bass player and pianist and now teaches electronic music, to explain the effect of the overwhelming sound. "Live music," he told me, "doesn't have the sonic capability to hit and vibrate you and force you to move." Because sound is so important for both live and electronic music, "the room is your instrument. Live bands want a room that doesn't have a lot of absorption, which deadens sound; electronic music has to have bass traps to control some of the low frequencies you can't get with live instruments."

Chris Annibell, a professor of electronic composition at Long Island University, was already playing the piano when he was in second grade, and he was a drum and percussion major in college; but, he says, "as a rhythm player" in a live band, "you're always a supporting character." With electronic music, percussion, he explained, is the star. "When people go out to dance for four to eight hours, it's very physical. A dancer's high is like a runner's high—connecting on endorphins . . . [the dancer] achieves a level of euphoria by exerting such physical activity."

I've experienced a similar kind of euphoria when the beat of a drum or a continuous rhythm increases the beauty of the colors I see.

Drugs can produce comparable responses. The anthropologist Wade Davis wrote in *One River: Explorations and Discoveries in the Amazon Rain Forest* about the effect of peyote on the music-color connection in an altered state: "Each audible stroke of the pendulum produced an explosion of color. The low notes of the piano produced a hallucination of violet, while high notes produced rose and white. And further, the effect of the piano was most curious and delightful . . . the whole air being filled with music, each note of which seemed to arrange around itself a medley of other notes which to me appeared to be surrounded by a halo of color pulsating to the music."

Take your pick: electronic music or peyote. Music played by live musicians is my drug of choice.

In 1996, I was honored as a "Living Landmark" by the New York Landmarks Conservancy, and I've played at the Conservancy's events ever since. Here, my vocalist and guitarist Roberta Fabiano is on the left, and my drummer and office manager Barry Lazarowitz is on drums.

Photograph courtesy of the New York Landmarks Conservancy

CHAPTER SIXTEEN

Social
Action

Dancing with Danger:
Yale in Mississippi

TRUMAN CAPOTE WAS STILL writing *In Cold Blood,* his Black and White Ball was in an unimagined future, and I was starting my first season at the Maisonette, as the world around us began to tip on its axis. The civil rights movement was under way, and as we watched television, we heard other noises that defined the times: guns, shouts, snarling dogs, police sirens. Many college students, among them a large number of Yale undergraduates and friends who had graduated around the same time I did, were traveling around Mississippi in the summer of 1962, advising Blacks on voting rights, and singing "We Shall Overcome." That might not seem like a lot, but it was a threat to the status quo. One volunteer told me that when he got off the plane from New York, the man who was sent to pick him up snapped, "Get in the car fast, or you'll be arrested." Volunteers were threatened and attacked; one told me about a hundred-mile-an-hour police chase. The local cops caught up with them, pushed pistols in their faces, arrested them, and jailed them overnight. Local pressure against the interlopers was so strong that even citizens who were against voter suppression kept silent, but the morning that the Northerners were leaving, the editor of the Jackson, Mississippi, newspaper, the biggest paper in the state, ran a front-page headline reporting on the Yale football scores, a subject of zero interest to his local readers.

"Radical Chic":
Lenny and the Panthers

IN THOSE YEARS, I was leading a double life: at night, I played for charity balls and private parties, where most if not all of the guests were White, dressed formally, and dancing the two-step. During the day, I'd be wearing blue jeans, seeing people who came together because of what they believed in, regardless of their backgrounds or education. I was involved, in whatever way I could, in the civil rights and anti–Vietnam War movements, and with new arts institutions.

During the late 1960s, the militant Black Power movement was grabbing front-page and television news, and the Black Panthers were the most violent group. They fought "the establishment" with arms; called cops "pigs," and engaged in firefights with police, which led to deaths. Huey Newton, one of the founders of the movement, was said to have killed a police officer; the author and political activist Eldridge Cleaver led an armed ambush of Oakland, California, police, wounding two. Cleaver was an odd combination; his collection of essays, *Soul on Ice,* was praised by *The New York Times,* despite his leadership in the Panther movement. His later political affiliations would be unexpected; he became a Republican in the 1980s.

In June 1970, twenty-one Panthers were accused of

plotting to blow up five New York department stores, New Haven railroad facilities, and the New York Botanical Garden. Members of the group known as the "Panther 21" had been jailed without trial for two months, and charged $100,000 bail each, which, of course, they couldn't pay. They were moved from jail to jail, prevented from contacting each other, and the authorities made it as difficult as possible for them to meet with lawyers to prepare their defense.

Even if some, or all, of the accusations were true, the Panthers had been deprived of the basic American right to defend themselves in court.

That injustice inspired Leonard and Felicia Bernstein to invite about ninety people, including Cheray and me, to their apartment to hear Panther leaders talk about their plans and philosophy.

It was no small act of courage for the Bernsteins to appear to be taking sides: the event could give the impression that they were sponsoring violence from their duplex penthouse. FBI director J. Edgar Hoover had described the group as "the greatest threat to the internal security of the country," and he was using his arsenal of harassment, persecution, incrimination, arrests, assassinations, and disinformation to destroy the movement. He also threatened another kind of danger. A power-wielding blackmailer and vengeance-seeker, Hoover held files containing secrets that could ruin careers and lives. His vicious obsession gave us even more reason to hear some of the members in an informal, private setting. The publicity about the Panthers had been ferocious. What did they have to say?

I hadn't thought about that night for a long time

until I was digging around in my boxes, and unearthed the June 8, 1970, *New York* magazine with the cover line, "A SPECIAL ISSUE: Tom Wolfe on Radical Chic," and an old outrage began to simmer. Maybe I kept the magazine because Wolfe mentioned that Cheray and I were there, and speculated that we might give a similar event at our house. (We didn't.)

The gathering was off the record, and Wolfe was a guest, yet he wrote a long, cynical, and highly stylized spin on the evening, trashing Lenny and Felicia, along with the rest of us. He damned us all, claiming that we were just socialites who had stopped by out of curiosity, on the way to better parties.

Lenny invited Don Cox, the movement's "Field Marshal" to describe the group's ten-point program. The demands were plainly impossible: Blacks were to be exempted from military service; all Blacks in jail were to be released; and the United Nations should hold plebiscites in Black communities "so that we can control our own destiny. . . . We want peace," Cox said, "but there can be no peace as long as a society is racist and one part of society engages in systematic oppression of another."

After we had heard from Cox and the others, some of the guests argued that violence wasn't necessary to effect social change. Others brought up Gandhi, but the Panthers had their own agenda. Peaceful resistance was not what they had in mind. After we had talked and listened, we were asked to make contributions for the Panther defense fund, and some did.

The supposedly private event was covered in newspapers, and even before Wolfe's "Radical Chic" article appeared, people read about it in other publications. The consequences were unpleasant, and in some cases damaging. Wolfe reported that I was playing at a party in Columbus, Ohio, when some angry "locals let [me] have it," which was definitely not as big a deal as he made it out to be. Lenny suffered more: a couple of his concerts were canceled.

Hoover obtained a list of the guests; opened or added to files on many of us, including me—he already had a thick file on Lenny—and made our lives uncomfortable whenever he could.

Wolfe also covered other connections between politics and Society, among them support for the movement led by Cesar Chavez to improve the conditions of California's grape workers, many of whom were barely being paid or fed, and were housed in filthy shacks without running water or electricity. A friend told me about a flight he'd taken from Los Angeles to New York, on which Chavez was also a passenger. Grapes were on the plane's menu and Chavez left his seat, walked down the aisle, reached onto plates, grabbed bunches of grapes, held them above his head and squished them. It was hardly bombing the New York Botanical Garden, which, by the way, never happened, but it was dramatic, and Chavez made his point. I wish I'd been there.

Some of the younger members of Society whom Wolfe targeted could have chosen to build careers on Wall Street, in top law firms, business, or publishing, yet they went to work for the Bedford Stuyvesant Restoration Corporation, established by Senator Robert Kennedy and two Republicans, Senator Jacob Javits and Mayor John Lindsay. Bed-Stuy was one of Brooklyn's most downtrodden neighborhoods. Residents were 85 percent Black and desperately poor; about 80 percent were high school dropouts. Houses were appallingly run-down. Banks redlined the area, disqualifying those who lived inside the invisible but well-understood border from being granted loans or mortgages.

Bed-Stuy represented the first public-private community development program in the country. Bobby, Jack Javits, and John Lindsay put together a powerful board of bankers, corporate leaders, and the heads of non-profit organizations; and people of the sort Wolfe had excoriated joined the effort, and took the subway to work in Bed-Stuy every day, when it was dangerous to live there and more so for outsiders.

Through the influence of bank presidents on the board, the practice of redlining was loosened; and IBM chairman Tom Watson set up a facility to make pallets in an abandoned milk bottling factory, providing much needed employment. Local leaders formed community groups to discuss problems and find solutions; and the neighborhood began to change. In the intervening sixty-some years, Bed-Stuy has become a center for economic empowerment, health services, culture, and affordable housing.

PLAYING FOR FREE

I PARTICIPATED IN ACTIVIST causes in the ways I could, often by playing at events without taking a fee. Most of my usual charity engagements were for established organizations, while these new cause-related groups were mea-gerly funded. The planners, who needed to raise awareness and money, couldn't afford to rent hotel ballrooms for formal dinner dances. In any case, dressing in black tie and evening gowns was out of sync with the goals, styles, and culture of their members. Instead, supporters invited potential donors to their homes. I would bring a trio, usu-ally a bass player, a guitarist, and me, and sometimes a larger group. Even though I didn't charge anything for myself, it wouldn't have been fair to ask the musicians to donate their time and talent. The organizations paid them as much as they could, and the musicians often agreed to work for below-union minimums. Occasionally, when they were as passionate about a cause as I was, we didn't charge anything. We played for Bed-Stuy; Citizens for Clean Air; Defenders of Wildlife; Friends of the Earth; and the American Place Theatre, founded by my former acting coach, Wynn Handman.

I was friendly with Rudolf Nureyev, the greatest male ballet dancer of his generation, who had become a world-wide celebrity after he defected from the Soviet Union. We often had lunch together at the Russian Tea Room, which was popular with people in the entertainment business, and just downstairs from the Carnegie Hall loft where I lived before Cheray and I were married. Nureyev's English was halting and heavily accented, but we talked about all sorts of subjects, from ballet and music to America, although he shied away from discussing the Soviet Union.

Nureyev introduced me to Arthur Mitchell, the first famous Black principal dancer at the New York City Ballet. In 1969, Arthur founded the now famous Dance

Theatre of Harlem, where he trained Black dancers, many of whom joined his company. He began by teaching in a converted garage in Harlem, leaving the doors wide open so people could watch what was going on. Some young men who saw that the male dancers wore blue jean shorts and T-shirts instead of tights felt more comfortable about giving ballet a try.

I played at events to benefit the Dance Theatre, and even wrote the score for a long-forgotten (including by me) jazz rock ballet. The Dance Theatre gained momentum in the midst of the Black Power movement, and as the dancer Djassi DaCosta Johnson wrote, "In moments of extreme injustice and frustration the most impactful art is born." Yet, as Virginia Johnson, the ballerina and artistic director of the company, wrote, "there wasn't a sense of militancy . . . around the idea of making Black people visible in this art form. It was more that he [Arthur] made dancers aware of the fact that they could define their own identity. That they didn't have to be defined by somebody else's perception of them."

I often played at the dinner dance benefiting the Metropolitan
Museum of Art Costume Institute when Pat Buckley was chair,
shown here at the party before the opening of "From Queen
to Empress: Victorian Dress, 1837–1877." In the early 2000s,
Vogue's editor-in-chief Anna Wintour took over, changed the
name to the Met Gala, and replaced music and dancing with
performances by such stars as Lady Gaga and Rihanna.

Photograph by Ron Galella

CHAPTER SEVENTEEN

From Society
to Celebrity

The Met Ball
and Pat Buckley's Bedroom

FOR ITS FIRST FIVE decades, the Metropolitan Museum of Art's annual ball to benefit the Costume Institute was held in the traditional style. I played at the party many times, and it was one of my favorite gigs, especially when the inexhaustible socialite and philanthropist Pat Buckley was the head of the committee.

Pat was married to my close friend William F. Buckley Jr., the brilliant conservative thinker, founder of the *National Review* magazine, host of the television show *Firing Line,* and author of many books, most notably his first, *God and Man at Yale.* I once called Bill "A National Treasure" and he responded that I was NT #2. When he sent me his books, he would always inscribe them "From NT #1 to NT #2." No one could ever call me conservative, but in those days people with opposing views could be friends.

One afternoon in the 1980s, Pat called and asked if I would come over to her apartment to discuss that year's Met Ball. She warned me that she was in bed because, she said, "I'm not feeling up to par, dahling, would you mind?" I laughed and made a comment like "Who was the last man in your bedroom?"

"Proust," she said quickly.

Aileen Mehle would be joining us, too. Aileen, who

wrote under the name "Suzy," was the most read Society gossip columnist in the United States. Bill once remarked that she "is known to a few dozen million people, plus the few who really count, as 'Suzy.'"

I went over to the Buckleys' apartment, and as Pat had warned, she was coughing and laughing in her deep smoker's voice, bolstered in bed by a jumble of pillows and surrounded by pads, notes, papers, and King Charles spaniels.

She hadn't been restrained in decorating her bedroom. The walls and furniture were covered in a bold bird-and-flowers pattern, and an enormous mirror, shaped like some kind of sea creature, hung over the fireplace. She said Bill would "die" if he knew how much it had cost.

When she wasn't "feeling under par," Pat seemed to stretch on and on. She stood just under six feet, and her style was, to say the least, dramatic. She applied dark gray eye shadow from her heavily mascaraed eyelashes to her eyebrows; and only she could get away with her hairstyle—short, dramatically streaked gray and blond, and wildly, if carefully, tousled. When she walked into a room, people looked.

Pat was internationally known, as an Australian newspaper commented, for her ability to "balance the high life with good works, throwing into the mix a wicked, worldly gift for friendship, a bold style and a total disregard for the politically correct."

From the 1970s into the early 1990s, when she became ill, Pat was ubiquitous. Charlotte Curtis, the *New York Times* social reporter, wrote, "There have been weeks along New York's charity circuit when it looked as if Mrs. William F. Buckley, Jr. was the chairman of everything." The *Times*'s Enid Nemy declared that the word around town was "Get Pat on a committee, and everybody will come."

She raised about $2 million a year at the Met Costume Institute Ball and the *Times* credited her with turning the party "into one of the most prestigious and in-demand social events of the New York season." The tickets initially cost $150; then the price jumped to $750 to keep pace with other charity balls. We were worried that it was too high, but "everyone" still came.

At the Buckleys' dinner parties, regulars included such notable wits as David Niven, Bill Blass, and Peter Grenville. Sometimes, when Bill felt like changing the mood, or got bored with the conversation, he would slyly gesture to me to follow him into an adjoining room, point to his harpsichord, and say, "You play the right hand, and I'll play the left." One night, he chose an extremely difficult piece, the *Goldberg Variations*. I said, "For Christ's sake, Bill, I can't play that." He smiled and remarked, "Practice, dear boy." He was damn good for an amateur, and we got through it, although quite a bit more slowly than Bach had envisioned.

"Society" was already drooping that afternoon at Pat's, but it wasn't quite flat on its back, and the two lively "birds" in the faux-bucolic scene were busy working on the seating plan for that year's Costume Institute Ball, and wanted my take. The ball would be held at the Met's Egyptian Temple of Dendur, which had only been open to the public since 1978 and an event there was still something of a novelty. The enclosure is glass-walled on the north, with a glass skylight, and bare walls and floor, and the acoustics were terrible. Two thousand years ago, the building had not been built to accommodate dancing to "You're the top . . ." I told Pat we could avoid the echo with a softer volume that suited the space. The trumpet players put in mutes; the drummer used brushes instead of sticks, and it worked out just fine.

"SUZY"

BASED ON THE NUMBER of cigarettes stubbed out in ashtrays, it looked as though Pat and Aileen had been working on the party for hours. Aileen was perched on a loveseat, with one of Pat's dogs on her lap and a coffee cup on a nearby table. Like Pat, whose father was a Canadian lumber and mining tycoon, she came from a privileged background: she was the daughter of an oilman. A tiny beauty, she was 5'3" and wore a size four shoe. Her hair was blond and curly; she highlighted her big blue eyes with eyeliner and, I think, false eyelashes; but her most striking feature was her wide smile and trademark red lipstick. She wore feminine and sometimes fluffy clothes; one night, when we were playing at a party in Texas, her dress was covered in feathers, which kept falling off and blowing around. I asked her to be careful that they didn't float into the instruments.

Aileen was the ideal columnist for a period that hadn't quite ended. As one socialite remarked, "Glamour was her occupation; she wrote about it and lived it. She was the social historian of her era." The *New York Times* reporter Sam Roberts wrote that "high society still preoccupied mass audiences as passionately as Hollywood stars did, and . . . the rich still delighted in tattling on one another in print."

Although she wasn't usually mean, occasionally Aileen couldn't resist the pointed quip. She called Zsa Zsa Gabor "Miss Chicken Paprika of 1914," and commented about Aristotle Onassis's yacht, *Christina O*, "I would love to tell you the precious mosaic swimming pool on deck was filled with champagne, but it wasn't. Everyone else was." I was invited to take several trips on that amazing yacht. One of its unique features was that the barstools were upholstered in whale penis skin.

ANNA WINTOUR'S PARTY

PAT BUCKLEY DIED IN 2007, and *Vogue*'s editor-in-chief Anna Wintour was appointed chair of the Costume Institute Ball. She renamed the event the Met Gala, and turned it into what has been described as "The East Coast Academy Awards." She eliminated a band and dancing, and replaced the ball with a dinner, highlighted by a performance by a world-class star.

Anna, who is one of the most powerful women in New York, in philanthropy as well as publishing, grew up in England with journalism in her DNA: her father was the editor of the *London Evening Standard*. She always had an eye on style; at fifteen she chose her signature haircut, a reddish brown bob that curves slightly forward at chin level with a perfectly straight part and bangs that just reach her eyebrows. Her look hasn't changed since the spotlight first shone on her when she was appointed the editor of *British Vogue*.

She described the reader she planned to attract: "I want *Vogue* to be pacy, sharp and sexy. I'm not interested in the super-rich or the infinitely leisured. I want our readers to be energetic executive women with money of their own and a wide range of interests. There's a new woman out there . . . she wants to know what and why and where and how." When Anna moved to New York and took over American *Vogue,* her philosophy was the same, and the magazine flourished: in September 2019, the issue ran 658 pages.

Under Anna's direction, a dedicated *Vogue* team performs the year-long work of organizing the Gala, which is held on the first Monday in May, the night before the show opens to the public. The publicity focuses on stars wearing spectacular costumes, who show up on television, the internet, YouTube, and in newspapers, magazines, and a special issue of the magazine; but what really matters is that the Costume Institute is the only department in the museum that is self-funded. With tickets at $35,000 and a table priced at $375,000, the Gala raised $15 million in 2019, which covered the cost of running the department.

While Pat Buckley's list largely consisted of Society figures, Anna invites important fashion designers and movie and other entertainment personalities, who share professional interests. Designers use the Costume Institute's 35,000-item collection for inspiration; as an archive of social history as seen through fashion; and a repository of some of their own work. The stars make a career-boosting splash on the night of the Gala by wearing clothes many of the same designers create especially for them.

THE EAST COAST ACADEMY AWARDS

I WAS CURIOUS TO see what the party at which I had played so often had turned into, so I watched the documentary *The First Monday in May,* which takes the viewer from inception to execution, and from there to promotion. The event is often compared to the Academy Awards, in part because it begins with a "red carpet" entrance, but arriving at the Met is not for sissies. Guests have to make their way up the intimidating stone stairs outside the museum, while a multitude of photographers and reporters jammed behind a barricade call out "Look here!" "Great dress," or whatever, to get their attention. Many of the women play to the cameras, blowing kisses, or stopping to pose. Inside, the stairway challenge isn't over. The biggest stars are photographed and videotaped as they enter the Great Hall and ascend the next staircase. I am the vice chairman of the Met's Musical Instrument Department, and I'm often at the museum, so the next time I was there I counted the steps: twenty-two up to a platform, then another twenty-two. In the video it appeared that nearly all the women (and the occasional man) were wearing shoes with five-inch heels.

No one would have thought of describing Pat Buckley's Met Ball as "The Super Bowl of fashion events," but that was how André Leon Talley, *Vogue*'s then editor-at-large, described the Gala in *The First Monday in May.*

After the party is over, at around 4:30 a.m., *Vogue* staffers choose photographs for a special issue of the magazine, with the cover line "Inside the Met Gala." There's also a coffee table book titled *VOGUE & The Metropolitan Museum of Art Costume Institute: Parties, Exhibitions, People.*

In 2018, the Gala was the centerpiece of a commercial movie, *Oceans' 8,* the story of an all-female gang of thieves led by a heist mistress played by Sandra Bullock. Their target was a $1.5 million Cartier diamond necklace, which they planned to steal from the neck of a high-profile actress, right in the midst of dinner.

"Heavenly Bodies"

ON ANOTHER VISIT TO the museum, I stopped in to see the 2018 show, "Heavenly Bodies: Fashion and the Catholic Imagination," which seemed to be a disconnect. But Andrew Bolton, the director of the Costume Institute, explained, "The focus is on a shared hypothesis about what we call the Catholic imagination and the way it has engaged artists and designers and shaped their approach to creativity, as opposed to any kind of theology or sociology. . . . Beauty has often been a bridge between believers and unbelievers." I agree: that can also be true of liturgical music. He said the exhibit was not intended to cause controversy and that he had consulted with Cardinal Timothy Dolan, Archbishop of New York, on some of his selections.

The costumes, he added, "include some with explicit Catholic imagery and symbolism as well as reference to specific garments worn by the clergy and religious orders. On a deeper level, it manifests as a reliance on storytelling, and specifically on metaphor."

As that's often true of many of the sculptures and

paintings in the Met's collection, which I've seen and admired for most of my life, Bolton's explanation didn't sound far off.

The fashion trends of the night appeared to be halos and trains, some of which must have been as much as ten feet long. Luckily, those who were wearing them wouldn't be dancing. If they had been, the scene on the dance floor: trains overlapping other trains, and men and women tripping, would probably have been the kind of unmitigated disaster that sets off so much laughter in the band (had there been a band) that it would have been hard to play a wind instrument.

"Heavenly Bodies" reminds me of a story I've been told by an impeccable source. In 2015, Lady Gaga, a devout Catholic who was educated at the Convent of the Sacred Heart in New York, was to perform. That afternoon, Emily Rafferty, then the president of the museum, attended the rehearsal and mentioned to Gaga that she, too, had attended Sacred Heart, and had been chairman of the board when Gaga was a student there.

Despite the fearlessness Gaga displays when she creates her many different public images, sometimes she gets stage fright. That night, she panicked. Forty-five minutes after she was to appear on stage, she was still frozen.

Emily made her way through the crowd, entered Gaga's dressing room, and asked if she could help. Because of their common experiences at Sacred Heart, Gaga suggested that they pray together. They did, and Gaga went on to give a brilliant performance.

"Camp"

ONE OF ANNA WINTOUR'S maxims is "If we don't have fantasy in fashion, then fashion will never move forward." Maybe that philosophy influenced Andrew Bolton's decision to mount the 2019 show: "Camp: Notes on Fashion." The guiding principle was stated at some length in Susan Sontag's 1964 essay, "Notes on Camp."

Sontag describes "the essence of Camp [is] its love of the unnatural: of artifice and exaggeration . . . which converts the serious to the frivolous." She adds, "The discovery of the good taste of bad taste can be very liberating." She exempts jazz from Camp music, although she includes the operas of Richard Strauss.

"It is," she writes, "the difference, rather, between the thing as meaning . . . something, anything, and the thing as pure artifice. . . . The ultimate Camp statement [is]: it's good because it's *awful.*"

If you ask me, which nobody is likely to do: "awful" is . . . awful.

Among the outfits on display were a peeled banana evening gown, a mini dress with a very short round skirt that looked like a merry-go-round, and flesh-colored full-body stockings on two mannequins. The man's had parts of his body drawn on it, including, of course, a penis; on the woman, a heart-shaped doily with a red heart in the center covered her "private parts."

An unsettling outfit reminiscent of Hitchcock's movie *The Birds* was an enormous purple fur (I think) capelike item, covered with a relentless swarm of many-colored butterflies that partly covered the mannequin's face.

Salvador Dalí would have loved it. So would members of the French coterie known as "Les Incroyables et Merveilleuses," survivors of the French Revolution Reign of Terror. Among the entertainments were *bals des victimes* held by young aristocrats whose family members had been guillotined. Some dressed in mourning attire; others wore black armbands. When they greeted each other, they made violent head movements to mimic decapitation.

As for me, I took a quick look and scampered off to the Musical Instruments Department, where I feel more comfortable. I've spent quite a lot of time there, enjoying and learning about the extraordinary collection of instruments from many centuries and all kinds of cultures. I've often thought of using some of those instruments in my band, as Paul Simon has done, producing beautiful results with South African music.

The *New York Social Diary* reported that Andrew Bolton said, "Camp tends to come to the fore in moments of political instability like the Sixties and the Eighties. . . . [It] is by nature subversive and a challenge to the status quo."

"We are going through an extreme camp moment," Bolton explained, "and it felt very relevant to the cultural conversation to look at what is often dismissed as empty frivolity but can actually be a very sophisticated and powerful political tool especially for marginalized cultures. . . . I think it's very timely."

What's "timely," of course, keeps changing. In 2020, for the museum's 150th anniversary, the show, "About Time: Fashion and Duration," was less dramatic, but from my perspective more interesting than "Heavenly Bodies" and "Camp."

The enormous book published in concert with the show contains images of sets of two mannequins, all dressed in black, wearing outfits from different eras, which the introduction described as "iconic garments, each paired with an alternate design that jumps forward or backward in time. These unexpected pairings, which relate to one another . . . create a unique and disruptive fashion chronology that conflates notions of past, present, and future."

According to the museum's press materials, "the idea is inspired by philosopher Henri Bergson's concept of 'la durée'—time that flows, accumulates and is indivisible."

I could say the same about music and dancing: the story of entertaining in the twentieth and early twenty-first centuries also conflates "past, present, and future," contrasting and connecting Tessie's White Ball to Truman's Black and White dance; the disco revolution; the Met Gala; and the charmed parties at which I've been playing throughout my career.

What Killed Society?

THERE'S A SORT OF conversational game in which people discuss "What killed Society?" The answer is *not* by changing a ball to a gala. By the last couple of decades of the twentieth century, doubts arose about what Society means, if it exists at all, and who, if anyone, fits the description. Are those who attend a traditional charity ball with live music and dancing more representative of "Society" than an assembly of guests whose shared professional or philanthropic interests bring them together? I don't think it's necessary to answer.

With all I've seen, and the places I've been, I've concluded that "Society" is a convenient fiction, one that depends on a kind of tribal exclusivity and exclusion. Those who are included define who makes the cut and what the word means from one era to the another.

One thing is clear: being called a "socialite" is no longer a compliment. I almost never hear anyone use the word "Society" anymore: it sounds outdated and arrogant. The requirements for entrance to groups at the top of the social pecking order are more likely to involve accomplishments and shared interests—although, inevitably, money matters.

In *High Society: The Town & Country Picture Album, 1846–1996,* Kathleen Madden wrote that Igor Cassini "took to task all those faint-of-hearts" who claimed that Society was dead. "In my opinion," he wrote, "the only way Society could be wiped out would be if all the earth were devastated in nuclear war. Even then, you can be sure that if there were only three survivors, sooner or later two of them would give a party and not invite the third. Then the twosome would then become the first 'snobs.'"

Madden got it right: "Society is, at any particular moment, in any one place, whatever one decides to make it."

As soon as I could work again after my stroke, we were back
at the Blue and Gray Colonels debutante ball in Montgomery,
Alabama, at which I've played for many years; I love the city,
and admire the Blue and Gray Colonels Association, which
provides critical social services, focusing on the arts.

Photograph by David Robertson, Jr.

CHAPTER EIGHTEEN

Peter Duchin
Is Back

Onstage Again:
The Viennese Opera Ball

THE MET GALA IS a singular event: there's nothing else like it; but traditional balls with live music and dancing continue to take place all over the country. One of the parties for which we've played for many years is the Viennese Opera Ball, among the last events in New York at which men wear white tie. Dad's generation called the outfit "soup and fish," presumably in reference to the first two courses of a formal dinner.

When I had my stroke, we had been booked for the ball at least a year in advance. We called the sponsors and explained that I was recovering, but couldn't yet play. The committee chairman kindly replied, "Your band knows exactly what to do. Why should we change now?"

I promised that I would show up and be onstage, but as the evening approached, I became increasingly worried that I would fall when I walked across to join the band. I was using a cane by then; yet from the wings, the walk seemed as perilous as wobbling along a rope bridge over a crevasse. I made it, and to lighten up my entry, before the band started to play, I briefly stood behind the woman leading the strings section, and pretended to conduct. That was an inside joke: I had met with the musicians before they went onstage, and they assured me that whatever I told them to do, they would ignore me. One of them quipped, "You mean as usual, Peter?" The band had played quite a few jobs without me while I was out of commission, but they made me feel that it wasn't the same.

I settled on a stool next to Ray Cohen, the wonderful pianist who was standing in for me, and with a big smile he said "Welcome home."

The party, which was held at the Waldorf, began when the honored guests, who included the president of Austria, marched in and took their seats below the proscenium and the band. We played another march for West Point cadets carrying the United States and Austrian flags, as the cadets ascended onto the bandstand and showed the colors. The guests stood, and Ray Cohen, with me hovering next to him, led the band in the national anthems of both countries. Next, enormous doors at the end of the room opened and a horse-drawn carriage pulled in, with an ancient driver wearing some kind of livery. He drew the horses to a halt, and two opera singers dismounted and sang a duet from a Viennese opera. The carriage may have come from Central Park, the kind that attracts tourists and lovers, but it looked quite grand that night.

When the carriage was driven off, we played the march from *Aïda,* as a dozen debutantes and their escorts arrived, were introduced and curtseyed to the honored guests, then whirled around the floor in a classic waltz. After that, they danced a graceful quadrille, taught by an Austrian dance master, whom I heard had been especially flown over to teach them. I can still see him bellowing—I think the word was "ATTENSHUN!"—as they began.

The late Bill Cunningham, the gently eccentric photographer and a good pal, was standing just below the bandstand. Bill covered most of the important social events in town for his *New York Times* column Nightlife. Sometimes he made it to a series of events in a single night. That was quite a feat: his regular mode of transportation was an ordinary bicycle. Bill gestured to show me exactly where he wanted me to stand, and took a shot of me standing in front of the band. The picture was published, with the caption "Peter Duchin is back."

GIGS

MY LEFT HAND UNCURLED, and as the fingers began to move, I became more optimistic. Yet no matter how hard I practiced, my brain still wasn't sending the proper signals to my hand. We were getting calls for jobs, and I needed a "left hand" to fill in the missing chords. Roberta and I came up with a plan: I would play the melody and improvise with my right hand, while she played the left-hand chords on the guitar. The arrangement isn't perfect, but it works. My band jokes that I'm playing better than ever.

The setup doesn't seem to matter, but sometimes I get frustrated, thinking, "Damn it. I've been playing all my life, and people can't tell the difference when I can only use one hand."

As soon as the news spread that I was back in action, I was booked for three of my favorite events: the benefit for the Glimmerglass Opera, which takes place every summer in Cooperstown, New York; the Blue and Gray Colonels

Ball in Montgomery, Alabama; and the New York Living Landmarks ceremony.

I've been involved with Glimmerglass since the beginning, when my friend Paul Kellogg started the festival and asked me to join the board. The Glimmerglass Festival is one of the highlights of the summer cultural season. The benefit, which is held in the winter or spring at the Metropolitan Club in New York, raises funds for the Glimmerglass three-months-long Young Artists Program. The young singers have the chance to perform in the chorus, and sometimes take small parts in the operas, with top professionals. They work on the productions, study with a well-known artist in residence, and each member of the program gives a recital. As a board member, I help the organization expand its vision and its campus, which now includes a state-of-the-art opera house, designed by the architect Hugh Hardy. It stands overlooking the beautiful Lake Otsego, which inspired James Fenimore Cooper, the author of *The Deerslayer* and other classics. The town was named after he came up with the word "glimmerglass" to describe the shine on the surface of the lake at certain times of day.

For more than a decade, I've played at the Blue and Gray Colonels debutante ball in Montgomery, Alabama. The event is a benefit for the Blue and Gray Colonels Association, which provides support for community needs and the arts. One of the debs is chosen as queen, and introduces the other young women, who proceed toward her with their escorts and parents. For their first dance, I usually play "Thank Heaven for Little Girls." After the formal presentation, the "little girls" usually disappear.

When they return, they've changed into more colorful and sometimes more risqué dresses, and that's the end of virginal white.

Back home, the New York Landmarks Conservancy ceremony honors New Yorkers who have made outstanding contributions to the city, and are designated Living Landmarks. Before the reception, I ask the year's honorees about their favorite tunes, which I play as they walk up to the stage to accept their awards and make their remarks. One year, Emily Rafferty, who had just retired as president of the Metropolitan Museum, told me she was going to wear a red dress. When she made her way to the stage, we played "The Lady in Red." For Mark Morris, the dancer and choreographer who started his own dance group, which is now in its own impressive building in Brooklyn, we chose "I Won't Dance." As he reached the front of the room, he winked at me and started to sing the lyrics. One of the honorees said in his speech that he was worried that being made a landmark meant he would have to stand around like a statue, while pigeons lit on his shoulders and relieved themselves. Having been honored by the Conservancy myself, I reassured him that, so far, pigeons have never bothered me.

Afterword

Gasping for Air

IN EARLY MARCH 2020, I was pretty much back to my normal life, out nearly every day, going to museums, restaurants, movies, the theater, and dinners with pals. I'd planned to have lunch with a friend on Friday, March 13, but the media was issuing warnings about a deadly and highly contagious virus, Covid-19, which had just begun to spread in the United States. More than 80,000 people had been infected in China, and nearly 3,000 had died. Italy counted 15,113 cases and 1,016 deaths. Milan had been hardest hit, and the city was under lockdown. The U.S. only had 2,204 confirmed cases and 49 deaths so far; but the count went up by 600 cases between March 12 and 13.

Even though the president insisted that there was little to fear, doctors were telling patients over sixty to get out of New York. The weekend of March 13 marked the beginning of a great exodus from the city by those who were lucky enough to have a country house, or knew someone generous enough to invite them to stay.

My friend and I canceled our lunch date.

It was just as well that I wasn't going anywhere; I woke up late on Friday morning and I was too tired to change from my sweats and T-shirt. Aside from fatigue, I didn't have any of the symptoms we'd already been advised to watch out for: shortness of breath, loss of taste and smell, coughing, and high temperature. I just didn't feel well.

That afternoon, I lay down for a nap after lunch. I woke up still feeling terrible. Since I'd had a stroke and a seizure, something serious could be brewing, so Virginia called our doctor. He told her to take me to the emergency room, where they ran some tests. Nothing alarming turned up and Virginia and I went home. No one tested me for Covid.

When Adelle came to work on Monday, I wasn't in the kitchen as usual, drinking coffee and reading the newspapers. At ten o'clock, my bedroom door was closed, so Adelle looked in. I was in bed, not quite asleep, but not really awake, and the room was dark. I still felt pretty lousy.

"It was time to pay attention," Adelle recalls. She told me I needed some fresh air; I got dressed, and we took Harper out for a short walk. I was too exhausted to go far.

Adelle decided to spend the week in one of the bedrooms in the apartment, and went home to pick up some clothes. On Wednesday night, she heard noises from my room and ran down the hall. The light was on in the bathroom, boxes and bottles were scattered all over, and the mirror on the door was broken, with bloody shards on the floor. I had somehow gotten back to my bed and was lying on a bloody pillow, with a cut behind my ear, and no idea as to what had happened. Adelle cleaned me up and told me to lie back and rest.

I still felt rotten on Thursday. I slept, barely ate, listened to some music, and read a little. I was worried, but

I was also too wiped out to do anything but rest until I could get my energy back. My only symptoms were that I couldn't keep my balance and I was terribly tired.

Friday night, I texted Adelle. "Are you there? Help me." I had fallen again.

The next day I sent an email to my coauthor, Patricia Beard. "I'm still very weak. Wish I could get over this." That was the last email I would send for two months.

Virginia and Adelle decided it would be a good idea if Adelle slept in my room on Saturday night. She brought in a pillow and sheet and settled into my father's old rocking chair. At 1:43 a.m., according to her watch, I got up to go to the bathroom. She heard me say, "Come on, Duchin. Pull yourself together," before I passed out. Adelle managed to move me onto the lid of the toilet, balanced me against the hamper; and opened the window. The cool air revived me, and with her help, I got back into bed.

I slept for a while, got up, passed out, and fell again. It was 5:35 a.m.

Adelle said, "That's it. We're going to the hospital."

Virginia called an ambulance.

For those events and much of what followed, I can only stitch together my recollections with those of the people who were around me. I do remember the paramedics coming up to the apartment with a wheelchair, because the elevator wasn't big enough for a stretcher. As they rolled me away, I chatted with them a bit, but I was thinking, "My God. I feel like an old man."

In the ambulance, I suddenly began to have trouble breathing. My oxygen level had dropped so low, the paramedics immediately started to administer oxygen. That was how abruptly I went into red alert.

FORTY-SEVEN DAYS

A FRIEND WHO HAD given a dinner party Virginia and I had attended a week or so earlier emailed the other guests the day I was taken to the hospital. She wrote:

> *SAD NEWS*
> Dear friends,
>   Peter Duchin is in the hospital in NYC and he tested positive for Covid-19.
>   I am writing to let you know because we were all together at dinner on March 10th.
>   Please stay safe!
>   Much love,
>   Kathy

The virus that had been lurking in my system had taken over. In the emergency room, the doctors told me they were putting me on a ventilator. I had no idea what that meant. I just thought it was to help my breathing. Adelle had handed me my iPhone and charger before I left, and I had just enough strength to call Virginia and tell her what was happening. After that, I was intubated and sedated for what would turn out to be forty-seven days.

I'd had constant, close indoor contact with Virginia and Adelle, and for the next two weeks, they were quarantined in the apartment. Each morning and evening, they would ask each other "How are you feeling?" Otherwise, they said, the apartment was strangely quiet, a kind of waiting room.

Doctors or nurses called Virginia every day with an update. She kept track, making notes on stickies. The reports went up and down, but for the most part, I was "Critical, but stable." I later heard that friends nervously called Virginia to find out how she was holding up, but felt uncomfortable asking her about me, in case the news was very bad. Some of my closest friends, and of course the kids, called her every day.

As the weeks passed, my younger son, Colin, posted regular messages about my condition on Facebook and Instagram. He later told me that sometimes more than five hundred people responded to the posts. It never would have occurred to me that so many people cared.

Virginia went back to work. Adelle came to the apartment a couple of days a week to do errands.

A rumor that I had died suddenly circulated via Facebook, Twitter, email, and phone, to the extreme distress of my family and friends. The story was quickly retracted and corrected, with effusive apologies. I was still alive, but the longer I remained "critical," the worse my chances were.

People later asked me whether I was ever aware while I was sedated and intubated. I do remember a couple of flashes. I recall having a large blue tube draped over my left shoulder, ending in my neck, and inserted somewhere near my mouth, but where? Through a tracheotomy I didn't even know I'd had?

After I was moved from one floor to another, into a kind of tower room with slanted light coming through the windows, I saw a brightly colored abstract painting on the wall. I know something was there, but I can't quite visualize it now.

I hallucinated a couple of times, as I had in the early days after my stroke. Once, I thought I was taken to a nurse's apartment, where a bed was set outside in a bower. The nurse made the bed, but instead of tucking me in, she led me into a room, where there were other women. One of them was sitting in an enormous stuffed armchair. She had me sit in an armchair, too, but it was so deep I couldn't get out of it. I remember thinking that the nurse told me she was going to Poughkeepsie, but she never came back.

On another occasion, I was moved outdoors on the way from one wing of the hospital to another. Lying on the gurney, I thought I was waiting for a photo shoot for the *New York Post*. I gather that was the only time I was outside for three months.

Eventually my oxygen levels increased. The doctors told Virginia I was improving. She was cautiously hopeful.

Six weeks after I'd been admitted, I was finally able to breathe on my own for a short time. The sedation was gradually decreased, but the oxygen was still administered through a tracheotomy, and I couldn't speak. I didn't know what was happening and I couldn't ask. I understood that I was in a hospital bed, but I didn't know where and why. I was trapped in my body, isolated and afraid.

My mouth was dry; the nurses gave me shaved ice and sticks with a piece of wet green sponge on the end to suck, and I was fed through a tube in my stomach. I dozed a lot, and I still didn't really grasp what was going on.

A nurse came in and said, "Welcome back!" I shook my head. She told me I'd had a bad case of Covid and it was "a miracle" that I'd survived. I could hardly believe it. I had no idea how long I'd been unconscious.

Another nurse who heard that I am a musician brought in a radio. After my stroke, I had listened to music I downloaded on my iPhone. Now I put in my earbuds, lay back, and heard whatever was playing on the classical or jazz stations.

I called Virginia as soon as I could talk. Hearing her voice after so many months filled me with joy and hope, and tears came to my eyes. Still, I was lying in a hospital bed, unable to move. Virginia sounded as excited as I felt; later, she told me she was crying. After that, we talked many times a day, sometimes by FaceTime, often just by phone, and I began to understand the fear and strain she had suffered while I hovered between life and death.

Doctors came by and congratulated me. When I began to get phone calls, emails, and texts, people said I was "amazing," "fantastic," and a "hero." That didn't make sense. Heroes run into burning buildings to save children; or give their lives on battlefields. Maybe my "heroic" act was simply to encourage people that it was possible to survive this terrible disease.

The Rip Van Winkle Effect

I FELT AS THOUGH I had lost an entire tranche of my life, and in a way I had. Iran could have bombed Tel Aviv and

I wouldn't have known. I thought of Washington Irving's Rip Van Winkle, who slept for twenty years while his beard turned white and grew until it reached his ankles, and who awakened to an entirely different world. My beard had only grown a few inches, but the speed of the changes I had missed was deeply disorienting.

I was stunned when Virginia told me that the number of Covid cases in the U.S. had risen from 2,000+ when I fell ill to nearly 37,000 in early May. I watched the news on television, and saw how rapidly the virus was upending society. On July 16, shortly after I was released from the hospital, the identified cases had reached 76,000. A year later, in the summer of 2021, the U.S. Covid count was more than 34 million, with 608,000 deaths. Worldwide, it was 188 million and more than 4 million people had died—numbers that don't begin to reflect the unknown or unreported tens of millions who have contracted the virus or died.

It would be five months before Virginia and I could see each other. The virus was so contagious that no one over eighteen was allowed to have visitors in the hospital. Even when I was released to a rehabilitation facility, visitors were forbidden. It was a dreadful time. I felt alone and helpless, although, for some reason, I was never afraid I was going to die.

I hadn't yet realized how many people around the country, like me, were on lockdown or in quarantine. At least I had the nurses and doctors and physical therapists to talk to and tease. In my self-appointed role as a combination of gossip columnist and social worker, I found out a lot about them. Occasionally a hospital psychiatrist stopped by to find out if I was going crazy. A good-looking young nutritionist came by and told me I had to eat more protein to heal my bedsores, yet no one there could fill my craving to be with family and friends.

I'm naturally gregarious, and I love people. At my boarding schools, teachers and other boys were always around; college was the same. On the barge on the Seine, we often gave parties and jam sessions and I always had a roommate, or someone who needed a bed for a couple of nights sleeping on our dilapidated Army cot.

After I put together my band, the musicians became a kind of family to me. When I lived in the country, we had a band picnic every year at our house, with lots of booze, beer, hamburgers, and music. We traveled together, and usually played in rooms filled with guests. Of course, people were around in the hospital, and they were kind to me; but then they moved on to another patient, and the same nurses didn't always appear. In the rehabilitation facility, I had conversations with other patients, especially when late spring and summer came and a few of us at a time were wheeled onto the roof. I could look across 72nd Street and see the house where George Plimpton had lived. I pointed out the house and told a woman in a wheelchair near me about him, but those contacts were fleeting.

During the recovery from my stroke, I had been most concerned about my left hand. After Covid, when the hand had been immobile for months, it had become much worse. Now, as I imagined the limitations of a life that might be spent in a wheelchair, my post-Covid worries seemed more challenging than my post-stroke concerns. I would need tough, painful, and extensive long-term therapy to rebuild my muscles, and even that didn't insure a full recovery. My legs were atrophied because I hadn't used them for so long, and my first priority was to walk again. *Then,* I would try to take care of that damn left hand. It was a sign of my desperation that when friends called, I didn't hide my frustration. I'd tell them, "I wish I could get out of this hellhole." Of course, neither the hospital nor the rehab facility was a version of Hell, but they sure felt like Purgatory.

The stroke had given me a fresh perspective about my parents and my life; after Covid, as the weeks and months passed and I lay in bed, dozed, mused, and dozed again, I began to delve further into Marjorie and Dad. Having fleshed out my mother's background, I took yet another look, and wondered if she would have been the warm and fascinating woman I had fantasized about. Maybe the person who told Cecil Beaton she wasn't sure she wanted to have a baby would have continued to lead the peripatetic life he described, and only passed in and out of my childhood between adventures.

My dream that Dad and I would have played duets on our two pianos, or could have had "dueling bands" between the Waldorf and the St. Regis, started to seem more fantastical. I briefly wondered again whether I would have had that career in the State Department and worked for the CIA, which I'd considered when I was in the Army in Panama, but I doubt it: music is in my soul.

I think of my Yale professor Harold Bloom, who wrote of "the rage for reading and rereading." In a way, I was rereading my parents, as I had started to do with books after my stroke when I picked up *War and Peace* and *Anna Karenina*—which makes me think I should go back and read *Middlemarch* again.

GETTING OVER IT

I'VE HAD FRIENDS WHO said they hated their parents. As soon as they were old enough, they only saw them when they had to: Christmas. Weddings. Funerals. Others still blamed their parents for their own inadequacies, problems, everything that had gone wrong in their lives, or in their heads. I'm a firm believer that, except in extreme situations, the job is to move on, take responsibility for oneself, and *get over it.*

Maybe it was time for me to stop idealizing Marjorie and criticizing Eddy, speculating about the great parents they would or would not have been—and *get over it* myself.

My focus was on the present. Physical therapy came first, but television news and phone conversations, which were my main conduits to the outside world, bombarded me with reports of chaotic national leadership and the malignant disruption of the processes and systems that hold the country together. The dark atmosphere of fear and uncertainty caused by Covid was exacerbated by the spread of that other disease.

The resulting economic hardships hit home when I considered the restaurants and small shops that were at the core of my neighborhood: the family entrepreneurs I'd known for years, whose stores were boarded up. I wondered where they had gone, and despaired at the thought that they would never return. Musicians called to tell me they were out of work, and were running into each other while looking for jobs. A sax player in my band died. I asked about his funeral, but there were no funerals: only ten people were allowed to congregate, even at an outdoor burial. Concert halls, theaters, and movie houses were closed. Musicians and actors were dispersed, waiting out the siege.

The heart of the country was breaking.

THE RESET

AS THE MONTHS PROGRESSED, many of us became numb to the death toll across the country. The dead seemed more like numbers than real people. One loss I felt strongly had nothing to do with the virus. I had still been under sedation when my old friend and Yale companion Peter Beard, the fearless photographer I had run into in the hospital after my stroke, met a dramatic end.

Peter had developed partial dementia and walked with a cane, the result of an old injury from the time a mother elephant stomped on him and broke his pelvis and a lot of other bones. He was now ambulatory, but often confused, and when he went out on his property at the far eastern end of Long Island, he was always accompanied by his wife, Nejma, or the woman who had been hired to care for him. One afternoon in mid-April, he told Nejma he wanted to check on a shed which he suspected squatters had been using. He said he'd prefer to go alone, and Nejma went back to the house to feed their cat and charge her phone. When she returned, he was gone. As dusk fell, a search party was formed, but there was no sign of him.

The temperature that night dropped to freezing. Peter was wearing a light fleece jacket. By the next morning, he was likely to have frozen to death.

Yet the man who swam in a crocodile-infested lake on a culling project in Kenya was famously indomitable. Police, neighbors, dogs, drones, and a helicopter searched for him for five days, without luck. Nine days after his disappearance, a hunter found his body in the woods, just outside the search area. I guess the police were so relieved, they neglected to ask what the man was hunting out of season. I'd like to believe that, when Peter knew he was nearing the finish line, he walked off to die alone, like one of the wild animals he knew so well.

As partial compensation for the shutdown of the arts, some live theater and musical performances, and museum visits were replaced by virtual experiences. The Metropolitan Opera held a virtual gala in the spring of 2020. The benefit took place while I was sedated, but it was livestreamed, so I've been able to see it. Peter Gelb, the opera's general manager, arranged for singers who had scattered to fifty countries to perform arias in their own homes, usually backed by recordings of the orchestra. The virtuoso finale, Verdi's *Va, Pensiero*, was performed by the full orchestra and chorus, with each musician or singer shown in a little box on the screen. The Met's house is the largest in the world, with 3,800 seats. On the first night of the gala, 820,000 people around the world watched. The performances were free, but viewers donated $3 million to the Opera.

On New Year's Eve, when the Met traditionally holds a gala at which I've played many times, the Opera held another virtual event: four singers performed well-loved arias, and ended with "Auld Lang Syne." I imagine some viewers at home sang along. A long list of supporters raised $2.6 million, which included a $1 million matching grant. The 2019 New Year's Eve gala raised $1.3 million. The Opera will return to in-person performances and celebrations; but maybe when those evenings are over, they'll be livestreamed for a modest subscription price; and once again, hundreds of thousands of people around the world will be able to tune in.

Other cultural institutions created virtual events. The Frick Collection's "Cocktails with a Curator" took place each Friday night at 6:00; each week a curator talked about an art object, from a painting to a teapot. If you missed any, they were available online. The Metropolitan Museum of Art held a series called "Curator's Cut" for members. I'm on the board of the Chamber Music Society of Lincoln Center, which offered online performances, and raised money for the Musicians Fund. Culture was being democratized, just as democracy was under brutal attack in Washington.

Creative people who would have been unlikely to find jobs in the fiercely competitive entertainment industry in normal times made up their own acts, and posted them on social media. Folks who couldn't go to the movies, concerts, the theater, or dine indoors at restaurants filled their downtime by watching and listening, and discovered talent that otherwise might never have emerged.

None of the musicians and actors I knew were making money, but the resilient human spirit was finding ways to interact, keep hope alive, and share beauty.

BACK IN ACTION

I'M WALKING AGAIN and playing the piano, but there have been plenty of changes in me, and in the outside world. It will probably take a couple of years to find out which will last. During the pandemic, we became accustomed to seeing people in intimate groups, often only two people at a time, and our friendships became deeper. I'm working on keeping that intimacy alive, with evenings like the first job I played after my stroke when friends held an all–Cole Porter concert in their barn for about forty guests. I brought a trio and a vocalist, we handed out the lyrics, and as we played, some of the guests sang and others spontaneously got up and danced. It was a lot of fun. I'm organizing similar evenings, featuring such composers as George Gershwin and Richard Rodgers; Paul Simon; or Bob Dylan, whose music transcends time.

THE WRITING LIFE

THE BOOK YOU'RE READING has been through a lot. When I started writing, I hoped that by describing how I dealt with my stroke, I might help others struggling with similar illnesses and disabilities. Then, during the long days resting in my room, surrounded by photographs of the parents I barely knew, I began to develop those new perspectives about who they were, not only in relation (or the absence of a relationship) to me, but as themselves, a man and a woman who were younger than my children are today. Thinking about Dad led me to the places and eras in which he and I have played; our association with "glamour" and "Society," and what if anything the words meant, or mean now. I enjoyed reliving many of those times, even as I reassessed how they fit into contemporary ideas about equality and small "s" society. Looking back has been instructive, moving, and sometimes painful. I can't escape the past, so my task has been to understand the life I've had; make peace with the tough times; celebrate the best, of which there has been a lot; and put the rest to bed.

My fellow musicians and I inevitably wonder how the patterns of collaboration and performance that evolved during the Covid era will influence music and dancing in the years to come—but whatever happens, I still have eighty-eight keys to figure it out.

THE END

IN 2020, THE YEAR of our trials, the poet Louise Glück was awarded the Nobel Prize in Literature "for her unmistakable poetic voice that with austere beauty makes individual existence universal."

When I read her lines below, I knew my book was finished:

the hope is that if you live through it
there will be art on the other side . . .

Acknowledgments

I am deeply grateful to Nan Talese, who believed in this book from the beginning; to William Thomas, president of Doubleday, who bumped up the release date of *Face the Music* to early December 2021, in time for holiday giving. On Nan's retirement, Bill Thomas assigned the thoughtful and superb editor Yaniv Soha, who gently and insightfully helped us to "brush up our Shakespeare." Our determined and effective agent and friend Laura Yorke backed us all the way. The publishing legend Michael Korda provided early encouragement and enthusiasm. Steven M. L. Aronson offered valuable editorial advice and support when it was most needed. The two portraits taken a few years apart were the work of the brilliant photographer Jonathan Morse.

At Doubleday, Michael Windsor designed the stunning cover; and Maria Carella's elegant interior design reflects the atmosphere of the story. Production manager Romeo Enriquez and assistant editor Cara Reilly moved the process along smoothly, so we didn't have to worry about anything except writing as well as we could. Marketing wizards Rachel Mollan, Anne Jaconette, Todd Doughty, and Michael Goldsmith persistently and creatively made sure that the book was "out there."

Thanks, as always to our families: Virginia Coleman, Jason Duchin, Courtnay Duchin, and Colin Duchin; Cheray Duchin; John Coleman and Sarah Coleman; David Braga; Alex Beard; Hillary Schafer; and "honorary Duchin" Adelle Dyett.

I will always be grateful to the doctors, nurses, and physical therapists at New York-Presbyterian Weill Cornell Medical Center and Mary Manning Walsh, with particular thanks to Dr. Frank Petito, and physical therapists Dan Tufaro and Rebecca Blumenthal.

Doctors Steven Frucht, Richard Friedman, Jill Bolte Taylor, and Concetta Tomaino helped me understand the effects of a stroke on a musician's brain. Chris Annibel and Dan Freeman shared their expertise about electronic music and clarified my understanding of the effects of what has always sounded pretty loud to me.

For their friendship, encouragement, and assistance, thanks to: John Alexander, Armin Allen, Scott Asen, Alec Baldwin, Keith and Ann Barish, Lia Bassen, David Berg, Jamie Bernstein, Marie Brenner, Jade Brown and Nick Moss, Wendy Carduner, Randy Cherill, David Patrick Columbia, Trudy Coxe, Bruce Crawford, Deborah Davis, Roberta Fabiano, Michael Feinstein, Toddie Findlay, Chip Fisher, Charlotte Ford, Molly Frank, Larry Gagosian, John Guare, Mayme Hackett, General Michael Hayden, Moira Hodgson, Philip and Alexandra Howard, Slim Hyatt, Lauren Landi, Barry Lazarowitz, Susan Lehman, Paul Miller, Pam Morgan, Susan Morrison, Scott Overall, Carmen Partridge, Renata Propper, Tom Quick, Kathy Rayner, Paul Romer, Steve Rubin, Robert Sakowitz, Lisa and David Schiff, Stan and Sydney Shuman, Sally Johnson Shy, Gabryel Smith, Jerry Speyer, Adrianna Trigiani, Bill and Melinda vanden Heuvel, Beverly Ware, Frank and Judy Wisner, and Jim and Elaine Wolfensohn.

Notes

Part One: Stricken

1   "Illness is the night-side": Susan Sontag, *Illness as Metaphor* (New York: Farrar, Straus & Giroux, 1978).

Chapter One: A Stroke of Bad Luck

9   "Music is a great example": Jill Bolte Taylor, email to the author, 2019.

Chapter Two: Fugues, Dreams, and Hallucinations

19   Many years later, George wrote: George Plimpton, "The Life of a Participatory Journalist," The National Press Club, November 21, 1990.

20   The saxophonist Gary Giddins: Geoffrey C. Ward and Ken Burns, *Jazz: A History of American Music* (New York: Alfred A. Knopf, 2000), xv.

21   "Jazz music celebrates life": Ward and Burns, *Jazz, A History of American Music,* xii.

21   The great pianist Jelly Roll Morton: Ward and Burns, *Jazz, A History of American Music,* 25.

21   "the United States of America": Duke Ellington, in Ward and Burns, *Jazz, A History of American Music,* vii.

Chapter Four: Zero Out of Ten

36   "Music is known to extensively activate": Kayt Sukel, "Different Kinds of Music May Aid Stroke Recovery," The Dana Foundation, June 27, 2017.

36   As I wrote in my first memoir: Peter Duchin, *Ghost of a Chance* (New York: Random House, 1996), 135.

Part Two: Absent Presences

53   "I was a son, parentless": Michael Ondaatje, *Warlight* (New York: Alfred A. Knopf, 2018), 229.

Chapter Six: Fragments

62   My father had a distinguished naval career: Eddy Duchin was awarded the Navy Commendation Ribbon, the American Area Campaign medal, the European–Africa–Middle Eastern Area Campaign medal, the Asiatic-Pacific Area Campaign medal, and the World War II Victory medal.

65   When Joe heard the lyrics: Richard Johnson, "Paul Simon Clears Up Mystery About Joe DiMaggio Lyric," *New York Post,* Page Six, March 7, 2014.

Chapter Seven: The Mystery of Marjorie

71   Searching in newspaper archives: "Motherhood Ends Life of Mrs. Duchin," New York *Daily News,* August 7, 1937.

72   My grandmother filed for divorce: *Eau Claire Leader,* July 9, 1921.

73   After the divorce, the two Marjories were left: *Eau Claire Leader,* undated clipping.

74   The caption under the photograph: *Chicago Tribune,* October 24, 1926.

74   My grandmother opened a second shop: "Home Beauty Course," *Indiana Star,* September 11, 1927.

75   Alexander Woollcott, the pudgy, brilliant, and acerbic: Anita Loos, *Kiss Hollywood Goodbye* (New York: Viking, 1974), 193–94.

76 And then there was my mother's exotic paternal aunt: Blanche Oelrichs obituary, *The New York Times,* November 6, 1950.

77 Blanche had three husbands: Letter from John Barrymore to Blanche Oelrichs Barrymore, undated, courtesy of Steven M. L. Aronson.

78 A 1926 article: "Miss Marjorie Oelrichs Speaks to New York's Brilliant Younger Set," *Washington Evening Star,* February 14, 1926.

78 Marjorie wasn't the only Society woman: Cleveland Amory, *Who Killed Society?* (New York: Harper & Brothers, 1960), 528–29.

79 My mother also occasionally wrote: Duchin, *Ghost of a Chance,* 29.

79 In 1929 CBS Radio hired her: *Hartford Courant,* November 26, 1929.

79 The series opened with "Part I": "Marjorie Oelrichs Tells a Story," *Hartford Courant,* November 6, 1929.

81 Marjorie became one of Cecil Beaton's: Cecil Beaton, Diary, August 1937, courtesy of Hugo Vickers.

81 For all her international experience, as Beaton would later write: Cecil Beaton, Diary, August 1937.

83 The other "Eddie" in question: New York *Daily News,* September 27, 1934.

83 The *Daily News* wrote, "The jovial (and shall we say plump)": New York *Daily News,* September 27, 1934.

84 Their marriage gave the gossip columnists: New York *Daily News,* undated clipping.

85 "Marjorie not only was special": Renata Propper, graphology analysis, summer 1999.

86 "It is as if all trees had died": Cecil Beaton, Diary, August 1937.

Chapter Eight: Eddy, Here And Then Gone

95 He became the concertmaster: "Harry Ellis Dickson, 94, Violinist and Conductor in Boston," *The New York Times,* April 2, 2003.

97 the Central Park Casino: Stephen Wolf, "The Night Spot That Roared," *The New York Times,* May 25, 2012; "Brilliant Throng Opens Park Casino," *The New York Times,* June 5, 1929.

98   More recently, the site had been leased: *The New Yorker,* June 8, 1929.

98   His friend Sidney Solomon was granted: "Says Park Bars Concessions": *New York Times,* May 25, 1929.

99   "a circular constellation": "Central Park Casino, Joseph Urban, Architect," *The Architectural Record,* August 1929.

99   As *The Architectural Record* reported: *The Architectural Record,* August 1929.

100   Within three years, Dad had replaced: George T. Simon, "Eddy Duchin," *The Big Bands* (New York: Macmillan, 1967), 179.

107   "I close my eyes, hum to myself": Simon, "Eddy Duchin," *The Big Bands,* 178.

107   Among the characteristics we have in common: Simon, "Eddy Duchin," *The Big Bands,* 179.

127   "Oh, the times! Oh, the customs!": one of the various translations from the Latin.

Chapter Nine: Becoming Peter Duchin

131   The next morning, *New York Times* television critic: "T.V.: Eddy Duchin's Son: Soldier-Pianist Plays Father's Theme in Sullivan Show Appearance," *The New York Times,* August 3, 1959.

133   "The fight is now an old one": Letter to Averell Harriman from Peter Duchin, Panama, February 1960.

136   "It is a great shame": Letter to Averell Harriman from Peter Duchin, Panama, August 1960.

Chapter Ten: Nightclubs, the Last Dance

146   "The New York scene was suddenly": Lucius Beebe, "Introduction," *El Morocco* (Privately published, 1937).

147   Sherman Billingsley: Facts from Ralph Blumenthal, *The Stork Club: America's Most Famous Nightclub and the Lost World of Café Society* (Boston: Little, Brown, 2000).

150   It reopened in 1964: "Nightclubs: In Old El Morocco," *Time,* December 25, 1964.

150   "It's nice to see it back": Frank Prial, " '21' and El Morocco, Two Legends Reopen," *The New York Times,* April 29, 1987.

153 Columbia wrote that Norban: David Patrick Columbia, *"Quest Salutes the 30th Anniversary of Doubles,"* *Quest,* April 2006.

Chapter Eleven: Glamour

157 "I know no art more atmospheric": Herbert Muschamp, "Playing for Keeps," *The New York Times Magazine,* March 13, 2005.

160 "The story of glamour is the story of": Virginia Postrel, *The Power of Glamour: Longing and the Art of Visual Persuasion* (New York: Simon & Schuster, 2013).

Chapter Twelve: A Society Bandleader

166 "Today, their son Peter holds the same place": Loos, *Kiss Hollywood Goodbye,* 93.

166 "propensity to music": Oliver Sacks, *Musicophilia: Tales of Music and the Brain* (New York: Vintage, 2008), x.

166 "We keep time to music": Sacks, *Musicophilia,* 282.

169 The drama didn't stop there: *The Newport Daily News,* August 20, 1904.

170 *Newport Daily News* described: "The White Ball Is the Event of the Season," *The Newport Daily News,* August 20, 1904.

173 "[He] remarks that WASPs don't like people": Louis Auchincloss, "Portraits," *High Society: The Town & Country Picture Album, 1846–1996* (New York: Harry N. Abrams, 1996), 274.

174 One of the books: Kathleen Madden, "What a Swell Party," *High Society,* 14.

174 "Attractive people, doing attractive things": Slim Aarons quoted by Kathleen Madden, "What a Swell Party," *High Society,* 100.

Chapter Thirteen: "The Debs' Delight"

181 Descriptions of Sally Johnson's debutante party: Sally Johnson Shy.

183 "the image of the debutante": David Patrick Columbia, "A Little History of the Debut" in Diana Oswald, *Debutantes: When Glamour Was Born* (New York: Rizzoli, 2013).

Chapter Fourteen: Truman Capote's
"Party of the Century"

190   As Deborah Davis explains: Deborah Davis, *Party of the Century: The Fabulous Story of Truman Capote and His Black and White Ball* (Hoboken: John Wiley & Sons, 2006).

193   He talked about the party so incessantly: Davis, *Party of the Century,* 150.

195   "It bridged old-fashioned coverage": Deborah Davis, phone interview, January 8, 2020.

197   "was branded from the inception": Deborah Davis, phone interview, January 8, 2020.

197   "No group mixed": Jack Dunphy quoted in Davis, *Party of the Century,* 244.

198   "He expressed some doubt": *Current Biography,* 1977.

Chapter Fifteen: The Discotheque Revolution

204   I asked New York University professor: Dan Freeman, phone interview, November 29, 2019.

204   "A dancer's high is like a runner's high": Chris Annibell, phone interview, November 21, 2019.

205   The anthropologist Wade Davis: Wade Davis, *One River: Explorations and Discoveries in the Amazon Rain Forest* (New York: Simon & Schuster, 1997), 56.

Chapter Sixteen: Social Action

210   FBI director J. Edgar Hoover: Tom Wolfe, "A SPECIAL ISSUE: Tom Wolfe on Radical Chic," *New York,* June 8, 1970.

211   "We want peace": Wolfe, "Radical Chic."

212   Wolfe reported that I was playing: Wolfe, "Radical Chic."

214   Nureyev introduced me to Arthur Mitchell: Arthur Mitchell was known as the first famous Black principal dancer at the New York City Ballet, but in the 1940s a lesser-known Black dancer, Arthur Bell, performed with the company before leaving to work in Europe.

Chapter Seventeen: From Society to Celebrity

219   Bill once remarked: Sam Roberts, "Aileen Mehle, Gossip's Grande Dame Known as 'Suzy,' Dies at 98," *The New York Times,* November 11, 2016.

219   From the 1970s into the early 1990s: Charlotte Curtis, "Pat Buckley's Benefits," *The New York Times,* November 20, 1984.

220   The *Times*'s Enid Nemy: Enid Nemy, "Pat Buckley, Writer's Wife and Socialite, Dies at 80," *The New York Times,* April 16, 2007.

221   Aileen was the ideal columnist: Roberts, "Aileen Mehle, Gossip's Grande Dame Known as 'Suzy,' Dies at 98," *The New York Times,* November 11, 2016.

221   *New York Times* reporter Sam Roberts wrote: Roberts, "Aileen Mehle, Gossip's Grande Dame Known as 'Suzy,' Dies at 98," November 11, 2016.

222   She called Zsa Zsa Gabor: John Loring, "The Original Gossip Girl," *Harper's Bazaar,* July 5, 2012.

222   Aristotle Onassis's yacht: Ibid.

223   "she wants to know what and why and where and how": Christina Larson, "From Venus to Minerva," *Washington Monthly,* November 2006.

224   No one would have thought: André Leon Talley in *The First Monday in May,* documentary, 2016.

225   But Andrew Bolton, the director of the Costume Institute: Lauren Alexis Fisher, "Everything You Need to Know About the 2019 Met Gala," Harper's Bazaar.com, May 6, 2019.

225   He said the exhibit was not intended: Christopher White, "Major Costume Institute Exhibit at Metropolitan Museum to Feature Vatican Artifacts," Cruxnow.com, November 9, 2017.

227   One of Anna Wintour's maxims is: *The First Monday in May.*

227   "The ultimate Camp statement": Susan Sontag, "Notes on Camp," 1964, https://faculty.georgetown.edu.

228   The *New York Social Diary* reported that Andrew Bolton said: Blair Sabol, "No Holds Barred: Talking Camp," *New York Social Diary,* May 14, 2019.

229   "These unexpected pairings": *About Time: Fashion and Duration* (New York: Metropolitan Museum of Art, 2000).

229   According to the museum's press materials: Channing Hargrove,
       "The Theme for the Met Gala Is . . ." *Discover,* November 8,
       2019.

230   Igor Cassini "took to task": Kathleen Madden, *High Society: The
       Town & Country Picture Album, 1846–1996,* 12.

Afterword

249   I think of my Yale professor Harold Bloom: Robert Gottlieb,
       "Harold Bloom Is Dead, but His 'Rage for Reading' Is Undi-
       minished," *The New York Times,* January 23, 2021.

Index

Page numbers in *italics* refer to illustrations.